PROPERTY
(248
#17008

Set design by Walt Spangler

A scene from the Broadway production of *Hollywood Arms*.

Photo by Joan Marcus

HOLLYWOOD ARMS

by CARRIE HAMILTON
and CAROL BURNETT

DRAMATISTS
PLAY SERVICE
INC.

HOLLYWOOD ARMS
Copyright © 2004, Kalola Productions, Inc.

All Rights Reserved

CAUTION: Professionals and amateurs are hereby warned that performance of HOLLYWOOD ARMS is subject to payment of a royalty. It is fully protected under the copyright laws of the United States of America, and of all countries covered by the International Copyright Union (including the Dominion of Canada and the rest of the British Commonwealth), and of all countries covered by the Pan-American Copyright Convention, the Universal Copyright Convention, the Berne Convention, and of all countries with which the United States has reciprocal copyright relations. All rights, including professional/amateur stage rights, motion picture, recitation, lecturing, public reading, radio broadcasting, television, video or sound recording, all other forms of mechanical or electronic reproduction, such as CD-ROM, CD-I, DVD, information storage and retrieval systems and photocopying, and the rights of translation into foreign languages, are strictly reserved. Particular emphasis is placed upon the matter of readings, permission for which must be secured from the Authors' agent in writing.

The English language stock and amateur stage performance rights in the United States, its territories, possessions and Canada for HOLLYWOOD ARMS are controlled exclusively by DRAMATISTS PLAY SERVICE, INC., 440 Park Avenue South, New York, NY 10016. No professional or nonprofessional performance of the Play may be given without obtaining in advance the written permission of DRAMATISTS PLAY SERVICE, INC., and paying the requisite fee.

Inquiries concerning all other rights should be addressed to International Creative Management, Inc., 40 West 57th Street, New York, NY 10019. Attn: Mitch Douglas.

SPECIAL NOTE
Anyone receiving permission to produce HOLLYWOOD ARMS is required to give credit to the Authors as sole and exclusive Authors of the Play on the title page of all programs distributed in connection with performances of the Play and in all instances in which the title of the Play appears for purposes of advertising, publicizing or otherwise exploiting the Play and/or a production thereof. The names of the Authors must appear on a separate line, in which no other names appear, immediately beneath the title and in size of type equal to 50% of the size of the largest, most prominent letter used for the title of the Play. No person, firm or entity may receive credit larger or more prominent than that accorded the Authors. The billing must appear as follows:

HOLLYWOOD ARMS
by Carrie Hamilton and Carol Burnett

The following acknowledgment must appear on the title page in all programs distributed in connection with performances of the Play in size of type equal to 100% of the size of the largest, most prominent letter used for the names of the Authors:

Originally directed on Broadway by Harold Prince.

The following acknowledgments must appear on the title page in all programs distributed in connection with performances of the Play in size of type equal to 25% of the size of the largest, most prominent letter used for the names of the Authors:

Original Broadway production by Harold Prince and Arielle Tepper.

First presented by The Goodman Theatre in Chicago, Illinois, on April 19, 2002.
Robert Falls, Artistic Director. Roche Schulfer, Executive Director.

Developed in part with the support of
The Sundance Theatre Laboratory and Robert Blacker.

The following acknowledgments must appear in all programs distributed in connection with performances of the Play:

Original music composed by Robert Lindsey Nassif.

"I'm Always Chasing Rainbows"
by Joseph McCarthy, Harry Carroll

"If I Only Had a Brain, a Heart and the Nerve"
and "We're Off to See the Wizard"
by E.Y. Harburg, Harold Arlen
EMI Feist Catalog Inc.

"Indian Love Call"
by Rudolf Friml, Otto Harbach, Oscar Hammerstein II
WB Music Corp./Bill/Bob Publishing Co./ Bambalina Music

"Rose Marie, I Love You"
by Rudolf Friml, Herbert Stothart, Otto Harbach, Oscar Hammerstein II
WB Music Corp./Bill/Bob Publishing Co./Bambalina Music

"Take Back Your Mink"
by Frank Loesser
Frank Music Corp.

"Taking a Chance on Love"
by Vernon Duke, John LaTouche, Ted Fetter
EMI Miller Catalog, Inc./The Songwriters Guild

"When the Red, Red Robin Comes Bob, Bob, Bobbin' Along"
by Harry Woods
Callicoon Music

"When the Moon Comes over the Mountain"
by Howard E. Johnson, Harry M. Woods, Milt Coleman, Ed Smalle, Kate Smith
EMI Robbins Catalog, Inc., Callicoon Music

"You'll Never Know"
by Harry Warren, Mack Gordon
WB Music Corp.

SPECIAL NOTE ON MUSIC

A CD containing original music composed for this play by Robert Lindsey Nassif is required for production and is available through the Play Service for $35.00, which includes shipping. There is no additional fee for the use of this music.

HOLLYWOOD ARMS was developed in part with the support of The Sundance Theatre Laboratory and Robert Blacker. It was first presented by The Goodman Theatre (Robert Falls, Artistic Director; Roche Schulfer, Executive Director) in Chicago, Illinois, opening on April 19, 2002. The Goodman Theatre production was subsequently presented on Broadway by Harold Prince and Arielle Tepper; the associate producer was OSTAR Enterprises. It opened at the Cort Theatre in New York City on October 31, 2002. It was directed by Harold Prince; the set design was by Walt Spangler; the lighting design was by Howell Binkley; the sound design was by Rob Milburn and Michael Bodeen; the original music was by Robert Lindsey Nassif; the costume design was by Judith Dolan; and the production stage manager was Lisa Dawn Cave. The cast was as follows:

OLDER HELEN	Donna Lynne Champlin
YOUNG HELEN	Sara Niemietz
NANNY	Linda Lavin
LOUISE	Michele Pawk
JODY	Frank Wood
BILL	Patrick Clear
ALICE	Emily Graham-Handley
DIXIE	Leslie Hendrix
MALCOLM	Nicolas King
COP #1	Christian Kohn
COP #2	Steve Bakunas
VOICES *(recorded voices only)*	Rich Little

CHARACTERS

OLDER HELEN
YOUNG HELEN
NANNY
LOUISE
JODY
BILL
ALICE
DIXIE
MALCOLM
COP #1
COP #2

PLACE

Hollywood, California.

TIME

1941 and 1951.

HOLLYWOOD ARMS

ACT ONE

Scene 1

1941. Lights up on the Hollywood sign looming in the hills. A young woman enters, stylishly dressed, her fashionable eyeglasses perched on her head. She has her back to us, seeing the sign as we do. She turns to face us.

OLDER HELEN. Hollywood ... well, to be exact ... in 1941 ... Hollywood-*land.* *("LAND" lights up, attached to the sign.)* Thirteen letters, fifty feet high. I sure never thought I'd wind up actually *climbing* it one day ... because my earliest recollection is living in Texas, with my grandmother, Nanny. My mother, Louise, had left me with Nanny when I was little and moved out to Hollywood. While Mama was living smack dab in the middle of "magic town," back in Texas, Nanny and I would go to the movies whenever we could. We'd sit in the dark for hours ... and watch all the pretty people up there on the screen. Nanny always said the picture show was a way "out," if only for a little while. I didn't know what the "Depression" was exactly ... I just knew everybody was in it. Before Betty Grable, Sonja Henie was my favorite movie star. She was this blond ice skater from Norway, and I just loved her. I had a pair of beat up old roller skates we got from the W.P.A., and I'd pretend to be Sonja, gliding over the ice, leaping and soaring and sailing through the air the way she did. *(Enter Little Helen, roller skating.)* I'd skate in circles on the old wooden floor inside the house ... *(Lights up on Little Helen, roller skating.)* Sometimes it seemed like hours ... *(Nanny enters. She's a handsome woman in her fifties.)*
NANNY. Helen! Quit that for a while, I can't hear myself think.

(Little Helen continues her circles.) For godsakes! You're making me dizzy as hell. *(Little Helen still skates. Louder.)* I said stop it. *(Little Helen stops.)*
OLDER HELEN. *(As Little Helen.)* I'm sorry, Nanny.
NANNY. I swear, Helen, sometimes I think you're pure-de deaf. Now, will you *please* take those off and go draw a picture or something.
OLDER HELEN. *(As Little Helen.)* I don't have any more paper.
NANNY. Well then, think of something else to do, but take off those skates! *(Little Helen sits on the floor and begins taking off her skates.)*
OLDER HELEN. Nanny was getting more and more frustrated. Mama wanted to be a famous writer and get to interview movie stars. Nanny would say …
NANNY and OLDER HELEN. It's all a pipe dream!
NANNY. *(To Little Helen, continuing.)* While your mother is out there in Hollywood, thinking she's gonna be the next Louella Parsons, we're stuck here in this hell hole.
OLDER HELEN. Nanny and Mama would write each other all the time. Nanny would tear open the envelopes, hoping there would be money inside. There never was, and she'd be fit to be tied.
NANNY. *(To Little Helen.)* On top of that, this bronchitis isn't about to let up. I've been coughing for five whole months. I swear I won't make it through one more San Antonio winter.
OLDER HELEN. Sometimes Nanny got so mad, she'd pick up the phone and even *call* Mama … *long distance … collect!* And then, it was Mama's turn to get upset. *(Louise, a pretty woman in her thirties, appears in her space.)*
LOUISE. Mama! I can't afford these calls! Can't you hang in a little longer? Don't you know how much I miss you and my baby?
OLDER HELEN. And then she would say …
LOUISE and OLDER HELEN. I swear I'll send for you soon.
NANNY. When pigs fly.
LOUISE. I've had a bit of a break from *Collier's* magazine … they want me to freelance and do a story on Cary Grant. Please … be patient.
NANNY. And while you're out there in Hollywood chasing down the likes of Cary Grant, we're sitting around here waiting for the next "norther" to come blow us off the face of the earth. And if I drop dead, what's going to happen to Helen?
OLDER HELEN. *(As Little Helen.)* Please don't drop dead!
NANNY. We're coming out there. I've managed to save just

enough for the train.
LOUISE. No! Not yet! I have to get on my feet financially!
NANNY. They have welfare in Hollywood!
LOUISE. Mama, please!
OLDER HELEN. Nanny won … So we packed up whatever we had, headed for the Southern Pacific and boarded the Sunset Limited. *(Blackout. In the dark:)*
RADIO ANNOUNCER. *(Fast and furious.)* Listen up Los Angeles! It's your friend Cahuenga Harry talkin' to you and I have got a once in a lifetime sale on the used cars of the stars! Yes, it's the unwritten rule of Hollywood: When you stop driving yourself, you sell your car to Cahuenga Harry! I've got Nashes. I've got Chevys and Buicks with rumble seats. I've got a Packard so perfect, so pristine you'll want to pull up a chair and eat your breakfast off the hood. Low mileage, new paint jobs! And one lucky starlet made it big after putting only two thousand miles on her 1939 Pierce Arrow. I dare you to tell it from new. No way! And every car on the lot under one thousand dollars. Stop dreamin', start drivin'! And remember, when a nobody becomes a somebody — they sell their car to Cahuenga Harry! It's the unwritten rule of the stars.

Scene 2

Lights up on lobby of a Hollywood apartment building. Dixie (the landlady) is behind her desk. She's reading a movie magazine. Nanny and Helen enter with beat-up suitcases, exhausted. Nanny looks around.

NANNY. So this is the "Hollywood Arms." Hmph. *(To Dixie.)* Excuse me. Where's Louise Melton's room?
DIXIE. She went out.
NANNY. Where?
DIXIE. How should I know, lady? *(Looks at Helen.)* You look sleepy, sweetie.
NANNY. Well she should! We've been sitting up on that old stuffy train for three days and three nights, with just crackers and water.
HELEN. *(Innocently.)* You had your sherry. *(Dixie guffaws. Nanny*

shoots her a look. Louise bursts into the lobby from outside.)
LOUISE. Oh thank God! I thought you were lost!
NANNY. Louise! Why weren't you there when we got off the streetcar? *(Helen ducks behind Nanny's skirt.)*
LOUISE. I've been sitting on that bench for three whole hours!
NANNY. Well, we sure as hell didn't see you. We must've walked up and down Vine Street …
LOUISE. *(Interrupting.)* Vine? Mama! I wrote you: HOLLYWOOD and WILCOX!
NANNY. Wilcox! I swear you said Hollywood and …
LOUISE. Oh Mama, never mind, YOU'RE HERE! *(Louise hugs her mother. Nanny hugs back, then takes Louise's face in her hands. Helen peeks out from behind Nanny's skirt.)* Oh my God, my baby … *(Louise reaches for Helen.)* Lookie here at you! Helen, angel, give me a hug.
NANNY. Give your mother a hug, Helen. *(Helen does, hesitantly.)*
LOUISE. *(Hurt, giving Nanny a look.)* My, you're getting real tall, just like your daddy! I hardly recognize you.
NANNY. Well, what do you expect, Louise? It's been two years.
LOUISE. *(Embarrassed in front of Dixie.)* Dixie, this is my mother, Mae White, and this is Helen, my baby.
DIXIE. *(Friendly, to Nanny.)* Well for Pete's sake, why didn't you say so?
NANNY. Because I'm not in the habit of telling my business to strangers, that's why.
LOUISE. *(Embarrassed, she smiles apologetically at Dixie and turns to Nanny.)* You must be exhausted.
NANNY. Well then, what're we standing out here for? Where's your apartment?
LOUISE. Mama, there's not enough room for all three of us in my place. I've rented a room for you and Helen right here off the lobby. I'll be just down the hall from you.
NANNY. Well dear Lord. *(Lights up on room 102.)* Just let me settle somewhere, please. The fumes on that bus alone were enough to knock out King Kong. *(They enter the apartment. It's a small room, with a Pullman kitchen.)* … and then walking all those blocks after we got off … just pure de luck, somebody didn't knock me in the head and kidnap the baby and the suitcase. *(Beat.)* Where's the bedroom?
LOUISE. It's right here, darling. *(Louise pulls on a handle in the wall and a Murphy bed comes down.)* See? It's a Murphy bed.
NANNY. A what?
LOUISE. A Murphy bed, Mama. I've got one just like it down the

hall. So when you're not using it you can just pick it up and swing it back into the closet and the apartment gets bigger.
NANNY. Where's the bathroom? Or does that come out of the wall, too? *(Louise leads Nanny to the bathroom. Helen fishes her drawing tablet and a pencil out of a suitcase, and sits on the couch.)*
LOUISE. In here, Mama.
NANNY. No bigger'n a stamp. Excuse me, please. *(Nanny shuts the door. Louise looks at Helen.)*
LOUISE. I'll bet you're hungry, aren't you Sweetie? *(Helen nods, not looking up from her tablet.)* Hey, lookie here what I brought for you. *(Louise retrieves a teddy bear from her bags and gives it to Helen. There is an awkward pause.)* Well guess what! I went to the store this morning and got all the fixin's for enchiladas! Your Nanny's written me how much you love them. *(Louise opens the icebox and removes a tray of food. She begins to grate the cheese and sprinkle it on the enchiladas.)* Tell you what, why don't you help me? I can teach you how to make 'em, too!
NANNY. Helen, bring me my purse. I need my phenobarbital. *(Helen grabs Nanny's purse and rushes to Nanny, who takes the purse.)* Thank you, baby. *(Nanny fishes in her purse, takes out the medicine bottle. Looks around.)* Honey, get me some water would you? I'm about to keel over. *(Helen dashes into the kitchen, picks up a glass off the counter and dashes back to Nanny. Louise walks back into the living room and silently watches this action.)*
HELEN. Here, Nanny!
NANNY. I don't know what I'd do without you. *(She downs the pill and belches.)*
HELEN. Feeling better?
NANNY. As long as I have you and my Christian Science. *(Nanny hugs Helen. Nanny sees the Pullman.)* Lord spare me ... that supposed to be the kitchen?
LOUISE. Mama ...
NANNY. Never mind, Louise. I just hope I'm not in for any more dandy surprises. *(Sitting on Murphy, exhausted.)* I've never been so whipped in my life.
LOUISE. I thought I'd make enchiladas, Mama, but if you're not up for them ...
NANNY. Well, I don't reckon I want to starve to death. *(Helen has returned to her drawing. Nanny has begun unpacking. Louise puts the food in the stove and returns to the living room.)*
LOUISE. *(Indicating tablet.)* Can I look? *(Helen hands the tablet to*

Louise.) Why, that's really good, baby! Will you look at that … a princess! *(Nanny is none too thrilled that Helen is already showing Louise her artwork.)* Can I have it? *(Helen looks at Nanny, who doesn't register one way or another, so she nods, tears out the page and gives her mother the picture.)*
HELEN. Here, Mama.
LOUISE. Thank you, honey. I'm gonna keep this forever and ever, 'cause it's from my very own little girl. *(She hugs Helen. Helen smiles.)*
NANNY. *(Breaking the mood.)* What do you hear from Jody?
LOUISE. Still at Olive View.
NANNY. Charity hospital. It's a wonder he's got a liver left.
LOUISE. It's not his liver, Mama. It's the tuberculosis that's keeping him there.
NANNY. And it's the booze that got him there.
LOUISE. *(Referring to Helen.)* Mama … *(Louise goes over to Helen.)* Your daddy's gonna come and see you real soon, Helen.
HELEN. When?
LOUISE. Soon as he gets out of the hospital. But I saw him the other day, and he's looking just swell. And honey, I want you to know that even though your daddy and I are divorced we're still good friends.
NANNY. Lord Louise, if only you'd married James Trail back home, we wouldn't be in the poorhouse today. He had class … and a bankroll.
LOUISE. Mama, Jody's doing the best he can. He's been off the hooch for a whole month now.
NANNY. Well, let's have a parade.
LOUISE. When he gets out, he's hoping to get a job at one of the aircraft factories since it looks like the war is really going to break out.
NANNY. We'll lose the war sure as hell, with *him* building airplanes. *(Beat. Louise changes the subject.)*
LOUISE. *(Looking at the drawing again.)* Helen, baby, I just can't get over this pretty picture. Why you're just a natural in the drawing department. Me, I can't draw a straight line, but I've got talent in other areas.
NANNY. The whole family's talented.
LOUISE. *(Chuckles to Nanny.)* Remember how you used to play "Maple Leaf Rag" on our old piano in the parlor, back in Belleville?
NANNY. *(Pleased at the memory.)* Lord …
LOUISE. *(Trying to cheer her up.)* Tell you what, Mama. After we eat, I'll run down the hall and get my ukulele, and we can harmonize

like we used to. Would you like that?
NANNY. What I'd like, is to know where our *next* meal is coming from.
LOUISE. Mama, I wrote you … about these couple of breaks that came up, to do freelance work at *Collier's* and *Pic* magazines. Celebrity interviews, Mama … movie stars!
NANNY. Well, thank God for welfare, that's all I've got to say.
LOUISE. You've got to start somewhere, Mama.
NANNY. You could *start* with the want ads!
LOUISE. I'm a damn good writer. It takes time, that's all. Don't you remember that story I sent you, the one I wrote on Cesar Romero? *(Quoting.)* "I come to PRAISE Cesar, not to bury him!"
NANNY. He really that good looking?
LOUISE. Yes, he's really that good looking!
NANNY. Wouldn't mind finding *his* shoes under my bed.
LOUISE. *(Laughing.)* Get in line, Mama.
NANNY. *(Belches.)* If I don't eat something soon, Louise, it's curtains. *(Blackout. In the dark we hear a radio announcer's voice. Throughout this, we hear the sound effects of screaming fans, cars, car horns, etc.)*
ANNOUNCER. *(V.O.)* "Ladies and gentlemen, the crowd here at the Grauman's Chinese Theater is bursting with excitement this premiere night, as the block-long limousines pull up to the curbside, and the world's most glamorous stars step out to greet the adoring fans. The klieg lights and flash bulbs from the cameras are so bright, why it looks like high noon out here on Hollywood Boulevard! If you've just tuned in, the red carpet, so far, has been graced with the beauty of Lana Turner, Linda Darnell and Joan Fontaine! Not to mention the dashing Tyrone Power and … wait! Another long black limousine has just stopped, and the crowd is going wild! This will be a night to remember … And it's only just the beginning!"

Scene 3

Lights up on 102. A few weeks later. Nanny and Helen have moved in. Murphy is now permanently down as Nanny has clothes, newspapers, magazine clippings, old peanut butter jars, bits of fabric, etc., packed into the hole in the wall that houses Murphy when not in use. There are old scarves and handkerchiefs hanging on the lamp shades, more newspapers and magazines thrown in the corners, brown grocery bags. Sweaters and dresses hang from the backs of chairs and in piles on top of the radio, the end tables, and the couch. The Pullman kitchen sink is full of old, cracked dishes. Empty jam and peanut butter jars serve as drinking glasses. The bathroom shower rod holds more clothes. Some of the cabinet doors don't shut all the way, as there is too much junk piled in to properly close the door. The "Big Ben" clock is in the kitchen cabinet behind a closed door, as the loud ticking makes Nanny "nervous." The alarm goes off. Helen stumbles out of "bed" (the couch) from under a pile of clothes. She shuts off the alarm.

NANNY. Helen, for godsakes, shut that cabinet door. That ticking drives me nuts. You know my nerves can't take it. *(Helen shuts the door. Nanny gets out of bed, feels her pulse, belches, and lets one rip. The fart is silent. She fans the covers on the bed.)*
HELEN. Peeeuuu!
NANNY. Well, there's more room out than in. *(Helen fans her face with her hand.)* Cut that out. It's not that bad.
HELEN. It never is, when it's your own. *(Stinky.)*
NANNY. Quit being so smart, you'll be late for school. *(Helen goes to the kitchen and starts making breakfast. Nanny ties a string around her waist and sticks a rolled up newspaper under it, pressing hard against her stomach.)*
HELEN. Nanny, why do you always stick the *Christian Science Monitor* up against your belly?
NANNY. So my insides won't fall out. *(By now, Helen has poured some cereal into a bowl. She takes the sugar bowl and begins pouring*

generous amounts over her cereal.) Are you cracked?
HELEN. What?
NANNY. *(Sarcastic.)* Oh nothing. *(Grabs the bowl.)* Except you've just used up an entire month's sugar rations! Now how'm I supposed to get this back into the bowl? I swear, Helen, we're at war! We have to space out our coupons or we won't have a thing left at the end of the month.
HELEN. I'm sorry.
NANNY. Just stay out of the kitchen unless you want to dry your hair in the oven. Okay? *(Helen nods.)* Now go get dressed.
HELEN. Mrs. Anderson says I can draw better than anyone in the class. *(Helen heads for the dressing room. Nanny makes a little sound and grabs a table for support.)* Nanny? What is it?
NANNY. *(Waving her hand across her eyes.)* Dizzy spell …
HELEN. *(Panicking.)* Here, lean on me. I'm not going to school! I'm going to stay here and know the truth for you.
NANNY. Oh, God … help me, Helen. Get my Christian Science book … *(Nanny swoons and lies down on the bed. Helen grabs a book and rushes to her side. Nanny clutches the book to her breast.)* Pray!
HELEN. *(Reciting very quickly, the words running together.)* "There is no life, truth, intelligence nor substance in matter. All is infinite mind and its infinite manifestation for God is All-in-All. *(Helen falters, forgetting the rest.)*
NANNY. Don't stop, Helen … hurry! *(Helen grabs the book from Nanny and frantically flips the pages.)*
HELEN. *(Under her breath.)* Please, God, take me first. *(Triumphant … finding page.)* "And Man is His image and likeness. Therefore, man is *not* material, he is *spiritual!*" *(There is a pause. Nanny lifts her head.)*
NANNY. You're my little miracle, you know that? I don't know what I'd do without you.
HELEN. *(Crying.)* I don't know what I'd do without you! Please don't ever die!
NANNY. I just need to shut my eyes for a bit. *(Nanny settles under the covers. Helen crawls up on Murphy and holds Nanny, rocking her back and forth.)*
HELEN. *(Whispering.)* Nice and easy. In and out. In and out. *(Lights out on 102. Lights up on the lobby. Louise and Dixie are hanging out by the cubbyhole mailboxes, Dixie sorting through the mail and putting it in the slots.)*
DIXIE. … so these two old men who haven't seen each other in a while meet on a park bench. "How's the wife?" one of 'em says. "I

think she's dead," says the other one. "Whaddaya mean, you THINK she's dead?" And the other old guy says, "Well, the sex is the same, but the dishes are piling up!" *(They share a laugh. There is a slight pause. Louise reaches in her purse and hands Dixie some money.)*
LOUISE. Here, Dixie. For Mama and me this month. I'm late. Sorry. And I'm three bucks short. You think you could bail me out? I'll pay you back as soon as I can. My interview with Cary's right around the corner, and Frank says it could pay even better than the Cesar Romero story.
DIXIE. Don't even worry about it, honey.
LOUISE. What can I say, Dix? You're aces, you know that? *(They hug.)*
DIXIE. So, Nick's coming over tonight?
LOUISE. I live for Wednesdays.
DIXIE. I caught him in that cowboy picture at the Chinese last week. He is so goddam gorgeous. He should be getting bigger parts.
LOUISE. Not much fun dressing up as an Indian, but it's a living.
DIXIE. How's it goin' with you two?
LOUISE. I can't remember the last time I was this happy, Dix.
DIXIE. And Myrna?
LOUISE. They hardly speak to each other. Soon as he gets enough money together, he'll get his divorce. *(Nanny's voice is heard from 102.)*
NANNY. *(Offstage.)* Is that you out there, Louise?
LOUISE. *(Rolling her eyes.)* Yes, Mama.
NANNY. *(Offstage.)* Where's Helen?
LOUISE. What do you mean where's Helen? Mama, she's supposed to be in school.
NANNY. *(Offstage.)* I had a spell. *(Louise leaves Dixie and goes to 102 and Nanny. Lights up on 102.)*
LOUISE. Oh for godsakes, you're always having spells, and nothing ever comes of 'em.
NANNY. I don't know what you're talking about. *(The air shaft by the toilet is lit. Helen climbs through the window.)*
LOUISE. *(Yelling to Nanny as she straightens up the messy apartment.)* I am *talking* about how she's scared to death to go to school because you keep "dying" every day. She won't let you out of her sight!
NANNY. Well if that's the case, then where is she?
LOUISE. Probably with Malcolm.
NANNY. *(Loudly, so Dixie will hear.)* Oh Lord spare me. That little hood's gonna wind up in the hoosegow.
LOUISE. Mama, hush. *(We see Dixie about to knock on the door.*

She holds off while Nanny rants.)
NANNY. He's a menace to society. Well, look at Dixie, the fruit doesn't fall too far from that tree. *(Dixie knocks.)*
LOUISE. Come in! *(She opens the door.)*
DIXIE. Hello, Mae. *(Dixie enters holding a child's strapped schoolbooks.)* I think they're playing hookey again, Lou, look what I found hiding behind the desk. *(Helen's voice comes through the bathroom shaft, where Nanny has left the door open.)*
HELEN. *(Offstage, yelling.)* If you don't quit knocking into me I'll beat the goddam crap outta you, Malcolm.
LOUISE. Found 'em! On the roof again. *(Dixie and Louise cross to the bathroom.)*
DIXIE. *(Laughing.)* Jesus, she cusses like a sailor, Lou!
MALCOLM. You lay a pinkie on me, turd face, an' I'll kick the livin' crap outta you!
NANNY. Well, it doesn't take an Einstein to figure out who she gets it from! *(Lights up on roof. Helen and Malcolm are on the roof, out of breath from horsing around.)*
DIXIE. *(Yelling up the air shaft.)* Malcolm! Get your ass down from that roof or I'll come up there and get you myself!
MALCOLM. *(Shouts down air shaft.)* You and what army? *(Malcolm and Helen giggle at this and run to the fire escape. Dixie returns to the living room.)*
DIXIE. Well, I'd better make tracks. *(Winking at Louise.)* Have fun tonight! *(To Nanny.)* Mae. *(Dixie exits.)*
NANNY. What's she talking about, "have fun tonight?" Where're you going?
LOUISE. I have a date with Nick.
NANNY. Oh dear God almighty! Are you crazy? Pinning all your hopes on an out of work actor …
LOUISE. He gets "extra" work, Mama, and when he does, the money's pretty good.
NANNY. Yeah, what … two, three times a year? He's a bum, Louise … a bum who just happens to already *have* a wife, by the way!
LOUISE. Not for long.
NANNY. … and you buy all that bull hockey!
LOUISE. He loves me.
NANNY. When are you going to wake up? If you were as smart as you think you are, you'd hook Bill Burgess while you're still young enough.
LOUISE. For godsakes, Mama, I'm only …

NANNY. *(Interrupting Louise, looking around.)* Shh! Louise! How many times have I told you, don't ever tell anyone how old you are! Men like 'em young, and don't you forget it.
LOUISE. *(Chuckling.)* Well, Bill sure as hell wouldn't care.
NANNY. What do you want to tempt fate for? The man's crazy about you, bringing you flowers, buying groceries …
LOUISE. I don't LOVE Bill, Mama.
NANNY. LOVE? Let me tell you something, Louise. "Love" has only gotten you in trouble. You "loved" Jody, and what have you got to show for it?
LOUISE. Helen.
NANNY. Oh for Lord's sake, don't go pulling that.
LOUISE. You "loved" my daddy.
NANNY. I *admired* Edgar Creighton. HE loved me.
LOUISE. What about all the others?
NANNY. I already told you, I never "loved" any of 'em.
LOUISE. Well, if you got married all those times for the money, how come we're not rich?
NANNY. Because it was frittered away, that's how come! Gambling, drinking … I never could get my hands on their bank accounts. I was a "woman." But all you have to do is crook your little finger and Bill would lay everything he's got at your feet, for godsakes.
LOUISE. "Everything he's got" isn't that much, Mama. He's got a steady job, that's all.
NANNY. Well from where I sit, that makes him John D. Rockefeller.
LOUISE. *(Dismissing, light.)* Well, then why don't YOU marry him? You always did like 'em young.
NANNY. Like talking to the wall. *(Giving up, Nanny settles on the couch. Louise makes tea, and brings a cup to Nanny.)*
LOUISE. What's on tonight?
NANNY. *Fred Allen.* Then I think Alice Faye's on later.
LOUISE. God, I love her singing.
NANNY. Give me Kate Smith any day. Now that's a voice. I love it when she sings "When the Moon Comes Over the Mountain."
LOUISE. Yeah, but there's no interpretation there, Mama. She just plants those size elevens of hers and blasts out every single song the same way.
NANNY. Well, Kate's got a BIG voice.
LOUISE. Kate is a BIG woman.

NANNY. They say all the truly great voices come from fat people. *(Louise takes out her ukulele.)*
LOUISE. *(Sings.)*
   YOU'LL NEVER KNOW JUST HOW MUCH I MISS YOU …
Plus, Alice is a looker. She'll never have to be buried in a piano crate.
NANNY. *(Snorting/laughing.)* Louise, don't do that! It came out of my nose!
LOUISE. *(Enjoying this, singing some more.)*
   AND IF I TRIED, I STILL COULDN'T HIDE MY LOVE FOR YOU
NANNY. Why she gave up my gorgeous Tony Martin for that loud mouthed Phil Harris is beyond me.
LOUISE. *(Singing.)*
   YOU OUGHT TO KNOW FOR HAVEN'T I TOLD YOU SO …
BOTH.
   A MILLION OR MORE TIMES …
(Lights out on 102. Lights up on the roof. Helen and Malcolm appear. They're dressed in homemade capes and are creeping SWAT-style toward one of the air shafts.)
HELEN. *(Whispering to Malcolm.)* Keep me covered. *(Malcolm flattens himself up against a part of the roof and carefully looks around.)* The coast is clear.
MALCOLM. *(They breathe a sigh of relief. Helen stealthily moves to another part of the roof, motions to Malcolm, who follows.)*
HELEN. *(Snapping her fingers.)* The binoculars. *(Malcolm produces a pair of beat up old opera glasses. Helen looks through them at the Mayfair apartment building next door.)*
MALCOLM. See anything?
HELEN. Wait a minute, I'm still searching for his window.
MALCOLM. You really think old man Parrot's working for Hitler?
HELEN. That's exactly what we're supposed to find out, stupid.
MALCOLM. Hey, watch who you're calling "stupid," stupid. *(Beat.)* I'm bored with this. Let's go climb the sign.
HELEN. Oh! There he is! Mr. Parrot! *(Malcolm jumps up and grabs the binoculars away from Helen. Yelling.)* Give 'em back, Malcolm!
MALCOLM. Pipe down … he'll hear us. *(Helen tries to get the binoculars, unsuccessfully.)*
HELEN. What's he doing?

MALCOLM. Looks like he just got out of the shower. He's wearing a towel.
HELEN. Lemme look!
MALCOLM. *(Sarcastic.)* Please?
HELEN. *(Emphatic.)* Please! *(Without looking at Helen, he hands her the binoculars over his shoulder.)* God, he's sooo wrinkly.
MALCOLM. Okay, my turn. *(Helen waves him off.)* Quit hoggin' it, an' let me have a crack at it, will ya? *(Helen hands him the binoculars, keeping her eyes on Parrot's window.)*
HELEN. What's he doing now?
MALCOLM. He's walking over to the coffee table … his towel slipped off … he's bending over … *(He begins laughing.)* Brother! Will ya look at that! Ohh, this is great! *(He hands Helen the binoculars. Helen looks through the glasses. Malcolm is clutching his belly and laughing. From Helen's physical reaction and change of attitude, we can tell she's seeing something quite shocking to her. Meanwhile, Dixie has come up on the roof, seeing the kids up to no good. She sneaks over and stands behind them. They are oblivious to her presence.)* Whaddya think of *them* apples?
HELEN. I … uh … he …
MALCOLM. Lemme look again! Come on! Please! *(Helen limply hands the binoculars back, only this time Dixie gets them. Both kids look up in horror. Malcolm's laughing stops on a dime. Soberly.)* I'm not doing anything!
DIXIE. And I'm Eleanor Roosevelt. You know you could wind up in the clink for less! Get your butt down those stairs, Mister. *(Dixie and Malcolm exit. Helen is left alone, confused by what she has seen through Mr. Parrot's window. Blackout. In the dark: We hear a siren. We hear the neighborhood air raid warden's voice coming over a bullhorn.)*
WARDEN. Don't be alarmed folks, this is just an air raid drill signaling a blackout. I repeat, this is a drill. All lights must be turned off. If you have to keep a light on, lower your blackout shades. We don't want to see any lights coming from windows. Do not go outside. The only people allowed on the street are your neighborhood volunteer air raid wardens. When the drill is over, you will hear three short whistle blasts, indicating the all clear sign.

Scene 4

Lights up 102. One week later, evening. Louise paces around the apartment. Bill Burgess is sitting on the couch.

BILL. *(Patting the couch.)* C'mon, Lou …
LOUISE. *(Reluctantly sitting down.)* Bill, they should have been back an hour ago.
BILL. Let's go to your place. We can hear them come back from down the hall. *(Louise doesn't answer him.)* Well, how about one little smooch, huh? *(He reaches for her.)*
LOUISE. Not here, Bill.
BILL. I'm not asking for the moon … *(As Bill tries to embrace Louise, she pours her drink in his lap. He jumps.)* Hey!
LOUISE. Omigod Bill, I'm so sorry! This is terrible.
BILL. It's okay … *(He stands up and begins to wipe his pants with his hands.)*
LOUISE. Oh, that's just awful! Look at that.
BILL. Please … don't worry about it, Lou.
LOUISE. I can't tell you how sorry I am.
BILL. *(Wiping his lap.)* It's okay, honest, this old suit needed to go to the cleaners anyhow. *(He begins to remove his pants.)*
LOUISE. *(Alarmed.)* What the hell are you doing?
BILL. Well gosh, Lou, I don't want to smell like a wino …
LOUISE. Oh for godsakes, give me that! *(Louise heads for the bathroom, pants in hand. She turns on the water in the sink and begins to wipe them with a wet cloth. Bill, in his boxer shorts follows. He stands behind her and puts his arms around her.)* Bill, cut it out. *(Pushing him away.)*
BILL. Aw, Lou … *(We hear Nanny and Helen in the hall.)*
NANNY. Worst movie I ever saw! Thirty-five cents right down the drain. I should have asked for our money back! Thank God. I thought we'd never make it! What a night! *(Louise and Bill freeze in their tracks. She shoves his pants at him and exits the bathroom, slamming the door on Bill. Nanny and Helen enter.)*
LOUISE. At last! I've been beside myself. Did you get stuck at the picture show in the blackout? *(Nanny and Helen march straight into*

the kitchen and begin removing silverware, napkins, and salt and pepper shakers from Nanny's purse over the following:)

NANNY. Oh, you wouldn't believe the hell we've been through! I just knew it was gonna happen when the sirens went off. No way to get home, and they wouldn't let us out on the street until that damned air raid drill was over! Four solid hours stuck in that movie house! I tell you, war is hell.

HELEN. We had to watch *Citizen Kane* … *twice!*

NANNY. Awful. Just pure-de awful! Couldn't have been Tyrone Power. I was bored to tears. Whoever said Oscar Welles is a genius is cracked. Couldn't make head or tail of it. Was he supposed to be in love with that sled, or what?

LOUISE. It's Orson, Mama.

NANNY. Besides, his head's too big for his body. *(She opens her purse and dumps the rest of the silverware on the table.)*

LOUISE. *(To Nanny.)* You're going to get arrested one of these days.

NANNY. *(High horse.)* The Vine Street Cafeteria can afford it. *(Helen produces rolls of toilet paper from her bag. Louise reacts.)* If we don't go overboard in the toilet paper department, we're set for another month.

HELEN. *(Proud.)* We hit every stall! *(Helen heads for the bathroom with the toilet paper.)*

LOUISE. Baby, Bill's in there. We were both waiting for you to come home.

NANNY. Oh my God, why didn't you say so? *(Nanny fusses with her hair and dress. Bill enters. He's dressed.)* Hello there, Bill! I had no idea you were here!

BILL. Hello, Mrs. White. Please excuse the way I look. I spilled my drink.

NANNY. Now Bill, since when do you owe me any explanations? And for heaven's sake, when are you going to start calling me "Mae?"

BILL. Mae.

NANNY. That's a whole lot better, isn't it?

BILL. Yes ma'am. *(To Helen.)* Hello, honey.

HELEN. Hi, Bill.

BILL. It's always a pleasure to see you and Helen, "Mae." And may I say how exceptionally lovely you look tonight? *(Nanny hikes up her dress just a bit to show a little more leg.)*

NANNY. Back in Arkansas, they didn't call me "the Belle of Belleville" for nothing!

BILL. Yes, ma'am.

NANNY. *(Beat. Wanting them to leave together.)* Well, it sure was nice to see you again, Bill, but I'd better get Helen to bed now. We're both worn to a frazzle. Say good night, Helen.
HELEN. Good night, Mama. Good night, Bill.
BILL. Good night, honey. *(Louise interrupts and steps further into the apartment. She picks up a box of candy and a bottle of sherry from the table.)*
LOUISE. Helen, look what Bill brought! A birthday present for you, and a bottle of sherry for you, Mama.
NANNY. *(Taking the bottle.)* Why, Bill. How thoughtful. Sherry is so good for the digestion.
HELEN. Wow. *(Opening the box carefully.)*
BILL. The big day's tomorrow, right?
HELEN. Yes.
LOUISE. Try to pick one with a creamy filling.
HELEN. Thanks a lot, Bill.
BILL. You're welcome, honey. Happy birthday. *(Guiding Louise by the arm.)* C'mon, Lou. We should let these young ladies get some shut eye.
NANNY. *(Faking a big yawn.)* We'll see you tomorrow at Helen's birthday party, right, Bill?
LOUISE. *(Caught.)* I was just gonna ask him, Mama.
BILL. That'd be swell.
NANNY. Now, you two lovebirds run along and have a nice night.
LOUISE. *(Grabs the bottle from Nanny.)* Why don't we all have a sherry, Mama?
NANNY. *(Desperate to get them to leave, she hands the bottle to Bill.)* Why don't *you* and Bill go to *your* apartment and have one? I'm about to fall out of my shoes, and my ears are still ringing from that blasted air raid siren. *(Louise takes the bottle from Bill and puts it in the kitchen.)*
LOUISE. Well then, Helen, why don't we all have a piece of that birthday candy?
HELEN. Sure, Mama. *(Helen and Louise are on the couch, they both peer inside the box.)*
LOUISE. *(Indicating the couch.)* C'mon, Mama. Join the party! *(Nanny and Bill exchange a quick look. It's hopeless, Louise isn't going anywhere.)*
HELEN. This one looks like it may have walnuts, Mama.
LOUISE. Oooh, I love walnuts. *(Louise tears into a piece of candy. Bill sighs.)*

BILL. Well, I think I should be getting along. Good night, Lou. Sweet dreams, Helen. *(Helen and Louise wave from the couch, happy as clams.)*
LOUISE and HELEN. Good night, Bill!
BILL. Mae … *(Nodding to Nanny.)*
NANNY. Good night, dear. *(Bill exits. Calling to him.)* We'll see you tomorrow at the party! *(She shuts the door. Beat. Nanny looks at Louise and Helen on the couch, giggling and eating candy.)* Are you out of your mind?
LOUISE. He'll be back, Mama. He always comes back.
NANNY. But for how long?
LOUISE. *(Interrupts.)* Things are gonna get better, Mama, you'll see. I've got a couple irons in the fire.
NANNY. The only iron you've got is Bill Burgess, and you won't *let* him put it in the fire!
LOUISE. *(Laughing, rising to go.)* Relax, Mama. *(To Helen.)* We've got a big day tomorrow, right baby?
HELEN. Right! *(Louise kisses Helen.)*
LOUISE. Good night, sweetheart. I'll see you first thing in the morning! *(At the door.)* Good night, Mama. *(She exits. Beat.)*
HELEN. What time is it?
NANNY. Time all fools are dead. Ain't you sick yet? *(Helen laughs. Nanny gets on all fours and looks under the bed.)*
HELEN. Who're you lookin' for tonight, Nanny?
NANNY. Clark Gable. *(Nanny and Helen giggle. This is a "routine" they do constantly. Nanny then goes into the bathroom to change into her nightgown. She closes the door.)*
HELEN. Nanny?
NANNY. *(From the bathroom.)* Uh-huh?
HELEN. Well, Malcolm was spying on Mr. Parrot's window last week, and he made me look, too.
NANNY. Are you crazy? You could get caught and wind up behind bars!
HELEN. He was naked.
NANNY. Malcolm?
HELEN. Mr. Parrot.
NANNY. What in the world would that old man want to parade around in his room for, naked as a jaybird. He oughta be reported.
HELEN. Nanny? What is that … "thing?" *(Beat. The bathroom door slowly opens.)*
NANNY. *(Not liking this.)* I don't know what you're talking about.

HELEN. I mean, I don't have one ... you don't have one ... Mama doesn't. What is it?
NANNY. It's none of your business, that's what it is.
HELEN. Why?
NANNY. You're too young, that's why.
HELEN. But I want to know what it is!
NANNY. *(Pause.)* That's his Roger.
HELEN. Roger? How come I don't have a Roger?
NANNY. *(Dismissing.)* You have a Suzy. Boys have Rogers. Girls have Suzys.
HELEN. How come?
NANNY. Don't ask me, that's just the way it is. Now enough of this filthy talk, it's time for bed. *(Beat.)*
HELEN. Nanny?
NANNY. Now what?
HELEN. Does Malcolm have a Roger?
NANNY. I'm afraid so. And don't you go looking for it. Now good night. *(Long beat.)*
HELEN. Nanny?
NANNY. Lord, Helen ...
HELEN. Will I have titties tomorrow?
NANNY. Titties! What are you asking about titties for? You're too young.
HELEN. But Ilomay's *(Pronounced "eye-lo-mays.")* only a month older than me, and she's getting titties!
NANNY. *(Pause.)* Well, it's not natural. She's probably fooling around.
HELEN. Ilomay's a good girl. She doesn't fool around.
NANNY. Well then, she probably rubs cocoa butter on her chest. You can make 'em grow that way, too. *(Nanny turns off the light. The dim glow of the radio light helps the audience barely make out shadows in 102. Silence.)*
HELEN. Nanny?
NANNY. Helen ... *(Not again.)*
HELEN. Fooling around. What does that mean, exactly?
NANNY. You don't want to know.
HELEN. Nanny ... PLEASE ...
NANNY. Hush up.
HELEN. Pleeeeeeeeese...? *(Pause.)*
NANNY. *(Quickly.)* The man sticks Roger in Suzy. Now go to sleep. *(Blackout. In the dark:)* You already wore your party dress on

your birthday, I don't know why you insist on wearing it now. We should save it for special occasions.
HELEN. But this is a special occasion! And I want to look pretty.
NANNY. You're nuts, you know that? Your father's not gonna give a hoot in hell how you're dressed. *(During the above dialogue we see a man, Jody, downstage, crossing to the door.)*

Scene 5

Lights up 102. There's a knock at the door. Nanny opens the door. Jody is standing there, a little nervous. A tall, thin man in his thirties, Jody is handsome, but worn from alcohol.

JODY. Hello, Mrs. White.
NANNY. Jody. *(He enters. He looks at Helen.)*
JODY. Hi, Punkin' Kid.
HELEN. Hi, Daddy. *(They look at each other.)*
NANNY *(Breaking the mood.)* Been quite a while, hasn't it Jody?
JODY. Too long, Mrs. White. Way too long. *(To Helen.)* Well, here now, let me look at you. You got so big.
NANNY. Amazing how that can happen in just three whole years.
JODY. Yes, well … *(To Helen.)* That's a very pretty dress you're wearing.
HELEN. It's my birthday dress. Nanny made it.
NANNY *(Almost overlapping.)* I made it for her.
JODY. Well, it's mighty beautiful, all right. And you look swell in it. I mean really, you look just swell. *(Helen is pleased and embarrassed at the same time.)* I was supposed to get sprung from Olive View in time to celebrate with you, but the doc wanted to keep me for a few extra days.
HELEN. That's okay.
JODY. Well, I sure have missed you. Your little letters and pictures cheered me up a whole lot while I was in the hospital. You sure can draw! *(Helen smiles, shyly.)* Matter of fact, I brought you a little something. I'm sorry I didn't have any wrapping paper … happy belated birthday. *(He hands Helen a paper bag. She pulls out a drawing tablet and some colored pencils.)* I hope I picked out the colors you like.

HELEN. Thank you, Daddy. *(Jody bends over and gives Helen a kiss on the cheek.)*
JODY. *(To Nanny.)* Oh, and here's a little something for you, Mrs. White. *(He hands her a dollar bill.)* I just wish it was more. I'm sellin' coupons door to door for now until I can get a better job.
NANNY. Thank you, Jody. *(Nanny takes the dollar and puts it in her purse, as she's getting her coat.)*
HELEN. *(Suddenly alarmed.)* Nanny, where are you going?
NANNY. There's a sale at Penney's. This dollar'll buy you a pair of pajamas.
HELEN. *(Warily.)* I don't need pajamas …
NANNY. Jody, would you watch the baby? Louise is out. Job hunting, I hope.
JODY. Why, Mrs. White, I'd like nothing better.
HELEN. I like my pajamas just fine. We can save the money.
NANNY. They're full of holes, Helen. They're practically obscene. Your daddy here can take care of you for a few minutes.
JODY. Sure, Punkin', we can catch up on things.
HELEN. What if you have one of your spells, like this morning?
NANNY. I'm over it now.
HELEN. You'll need me to be with you!
NANNY. Will you stop being such a little worry wart? I'm fine.
HELEN. I'm going with you.
NANNY. Don't be ridiculous. You stay here with your father. I'm perfectly fine. I'll be back before you know it. *(Nanny kisses Helen and is out the door. Helen yells at the door.)*
HELEN. What if you have a heart attack! You need me there to pray for you! *(Helen turns to Jody.)* I'm going with her. *(Helen heads for the door. Jody stops her.)*
JODY. Helen honey, she's fine.
HELEN. You don't understand! I have to be with her in case something happens! She's not at all well, you know! *(She sees the bottle of phenobarbitals on the bed table and grabs it.)* Look! Look! She might need her pills!
JODY. Punkin', your Nanny'll be back before you can say "Jack Robinson." I promise.
HELEN. Jack Robinson! Jack Robinson! *(Jody's between Helen and the door.)*
JODY. Honey, please try to calm down … *(Helen grabs the Bible and wheels around out of Jody's grasp, diving under Murphy.)*
HELEN. In the name of the Bible! Bring her back! Please God,

Please God, pleasegod, pleasegodpleasegodpleasegod ... *(With some effort, Jody gets down on all fours, talking to Helen under the bed.)*
JODY. Helen, now this is really silly. Cut it out. Can't we just visit a little? It's been so long.
HELEN. Please, Nanny! Please don't die!
JODY. Stop this, right now!
HELEN. Matthew, Mark, Luke, John! Mary Baker Eddy! SOMEBODY!
JODY. All right, that's enough! I thought you were a big girl, but maybe I was wrong. You're acting like a little baby.
(Jody, still on all fours, reaches for Helen, and she kicks at his hand.) Dammit! You stop this right now! Do you hear me, young lady? I said STOP! *(By now, he's out of breath and begins to cough uncontrollably. Helen seizes the opportunity and bolts out the door.)*
HELEN. *(As she's running out.)* Nanny! Wait for me! Wait! I'm coming! Nanny! *(Jody's cough is subsiding. He looks up and sees the open door. He rises and exits slowly. Blackout.)*

Scene 6

The lights dim up in 102 — one week later. We see Helen spreading newspapers on the floor, and beginning to walk back and forth on them. Lights full up.

NANNY. Now jump up and down.
HELEN. *(Jumping.)* I've been marching around in these god-durn shoes for TWO WHOLE DAYS!
NANNY. And you're gonna *keep* marching until I'm sure they're not gonna give you blisters. Stay on the newspaper! I can't take 'em back to Thom McAnn's if you get the soles dirty!
HELEN. They *always* give me blisters. They're always too big.
NANNY. That's so you can grow into them.
HELEN. When are we ever gonna get any that fit?
NANNY. Soon as I marry J.P. Morgan.
HELEN. I'm hungry.
NANNY. There's salmon balls in the ice box.
HELEN. I'm not that hungry.

NANNY. Don't get smart. We can get some candy at the picture show. Now go put on your old shoes. *(Helen starts to step off the newspaper.)* Stop that! On the paper! On the paper! Where in God's name is your head? *(Helen jumps back on the newspaper, sits on the floor and begins to take off the new shoes.)* Hurry up! I don't want to miss Keno night. *(Louise bursts into 102, wearing her coat. She carries a bag from the drugstore.)*
LOUISE. Our money worries will soon be history, ladies!
NANNY. *(Excited.)* Did you get the job?
LOUISE. No. BUT ... *(To Nanny.)* Your brilliant daughter, *(To Helen.)* And your brilliant Mama has just mailed in the winning entry to the Roy Rogers "Name Trigger's Brand New Son" contest!
NANNY. Oh for godsakes, Louise, not another damn contest.
HELEN. What is it, Mama? What is it!
NANNY. *(To Louise.)* You are pure-de cracked, Louise. Here you should be out pounding the pavement looking for a job.
LOUISE. I have a job, Mama. I'm a writer.
NANNY. I'm talking about a REAL job.
HELEN. What'd you name him, Mama? MAMA!
LOUISE. *(Teasing Helen.)* No, I said you have to guess ...
HELEN. Pleeeassseee.
LOUISE. *(Pausing for effect.)* "Bullet"! It's "Bullet"! Get it? Bullet out of Trigger! Trigger's little Bullet! Goddam, Roy's gonna croak when he reads it!
HELEN. Oh Mama, it's inspired!
LOUISE. *(Indicating Nanny.)* And what do we hear from this corner?
NANNY. *(Giving up.)* It's okay.
LOUISE. Okay? Okay? It's perfect! All we have to do is wait for Roy Rogers to go through all the crap he's gonna get, and then when he gets to my envelope, TA DA! Pay dirt! *(Louise twirls Helen around.)* Yessireebob, easy street! C'mon, baby. Help your Mama get gorgeous. *(She starts taking cosmetics out of the bag.)*
NANNY. *(Getting her coat and purse.)* We're going to the Vogue. How many times do I have to tell you, Helen, the prices go up at six!
LOUISE. *(Laughing.)* Oh Mama, I love it. Here you rag on me, and you can't *wait* to get to gambling night at the Vogue! When was the last time *you* won anything, huh?
NANNY. Well, at least I get a Nelson Eddy movie out of it. *(Helen is looking at the cosmetics. Re: cosmetics, suspicious.)* And just what is all this you spent good money for?
LOUISE. Nick.

NANNY. Nick!?
LOUISE. Yes, Nick. We're going to Musso's for a steak.
NANNY. Oh for godsakes, we're going to lose Bill Burgess! When are you ever gonna come down to earth? He can provide for us.
LOUISE. I can't make myself love him.
NANNY. Why not? At least he's American.
LOUISE. What's that supposed to mean?
NANNY. You know perfectly well. Nick's Italian. They can't be trusted.
LOUISE. *(Laughing at Nanny.)* It's almost six, Mama.
NANNY. Helen! Come *on!*
HELEN. I wanna help Mama get gorgeous.
NANNY. Fine. *(Nanny exits, slamming the door behind her.)*
HELEN. Maybe I should've gone with her.
LOUISE. Baby, don't worry. She'll forget all about it as soon as she gets her Keno card. *(Louise takes off her coat, revealing a new dress.)* Well, whaddya think?
HELEN. *(Impressed.)* Oh, Mama!
LOUISE. On sale at Lerner's … I didn't dare let the old lady see it, or I'd never hear the end of it … *(Twirling around.)* You really like it?
HELEN. It's beautiful!
LOUISE. C'mon, let's get to work! *(Louise clears the junk off the coffee table and lays out the cosmetics:)* Mascara, lipstick, leg make-up, eyebrow pencil. *(She begins applying the leg makeup. Singing.)*
 HERE I GO AGAIN
 I HEAR THOSE TRUMPETS BLOW AGAIN
 ALL AGLOW AGAIN
 TAKIN' A CHANCE ON LOVE …
HELEN. Oh Mama, you really do sound like Alice Faye!
LOUISE. Baby, things are gonna change around here, I can feel it. *(Helen nods, although not sure what her mother is talking about.)* Even though things didn't work out with me and your daddy, I loved him very much. You know that, right? He's a good man, Helen … just weak as hell. *(Helen nods again.)* Draw the seams for me? *(Louise hands Helen an eyebrow pencil. She begins drawing seams up the back of her mother's made-up legs. Louise pours herself a short drink. She begins applying mascara. Helen watches intently.)* Well, I haven't loved anyone like Jody since then … until Nick. And your Nanny will learn to love him, too. He just needs to get out of his current situation and get us all into a nice house somewhere.
HELEN. A house, Mama? Really?

LOUISE. With a yard and swings! And palm trees down the sidewalk. And Nick'll take us to all the big Hollywood premieres, and we'll walk down that long red carpet, and everyone'll look us and say: My, who is that gorgeous woman? And who is that adorable little girl with her? *(Helen laughs hysterically, as Louise tickles and hugs her. A quirky, fun car honking is heard.)* Oh, my purse! Where's my purse? *(The car honks again.)* Hold your horses! I'm coming, I'm coming!
HELEN. *(Handing it to her.)* Here, Mama!
LOUISE. How do I look, baby?
HELEN. Just like Joan Crawford. Only better! *(Blackout.)*

Scene 7

Lights up on the apartment. Louise is in the bathroom at the sink, with the door open. Nanny is in the kitchen putting away a few groceries. They are in the middle of an argument.

NANNY. … a disgrace and a damn fool, that's what you are.
LOUISE. Please, Mama …
NANNY. Just how are we supposed to feed another mouth, tell me that, will you? "Nick was gonna get a divorce. Nick was gonna leave his wife." Well, look around, Missy. See him anywhere?
LOUISE. Let up. Please let up.
NANNY. You thought you could trap him this way.
LOUISE. That's not true.
NANNY. *(Ranting.)* Flew the coop when he found out, didn't he? Mark my words, you can kiss Bill Burgess goodbye. *(Louise pours herself a healthy shot and drinks.)*
LOUISE. Mama, please …
NANNY. If he ever gets wind of this, there goes our meal ticket. We'll just have to do something about this before it's too late. *(Louise enters from the bathroom with a drink in her hand.)*
LOUISE. *(Deadly.)* Now you listen to me, old lady. This is MY baby. And nobody's gonna take it away from me.
NANNY. Louise, use your head.
LOUISE. NO! I don't want to hear it. You took Helen away from

31

me, and I'm not gonna let you take this one.
NANNY. I took Helen! That's a good one. You abandoned her!
LOUISE. You turned her against me!
NANNY. You did that all by yourself!
LOUISE. Leave. Me. Alone.
NANNY. I don't know how I'm going to hold my head up around here. You're a scandal.
LOUISE. *(Exploding.)* You're a swell one to talk about somebody's reputation after all you put me through when I was a kid.
NANNY. Here we go again!
LOUISE. *(Overlapping, on a roll.)* We can *all* take a back seat to you in the "man department," Mama.
NANNY. That's enough, Louise.
LOUISE. Hell, Mama. I never knew what I'd find coming out of your room when I came home from school. Why, I'd just get used to one "Daddy" when the next thing I know … poof! He'd been replaced. Usually with a younger model.
NANNY. You're drunk.
LOUISE. You bet! I'm drunk and you're a hypocrite!
NANNY. Stop it …
LOUISE. Six husbands, Mama! SIX!
NANNY. *(Afraid someone might overhear.)* Shut your mouth, Louise!
LOUISE. And God only knows how many others you screwed around with, for whatever you could get out of them!
NANNY. My heart …
LOUISE. What heart? You can dish it out, but you can't take it, can you? *(Nanny starts to have a "spell.")*
NANNY. God help me, I'm about to die.
LOUISE. You're not about to die. You're too mean to die!
NANNY. Louise, for godsakes, stop this!
LOUISE. And the worst part, the *worst* … you actually *brag* that you never loved any of 'em.
NANNY. Any more than that rat loved you? *(There is a pause. The two women are spent.)*
LOUISE. You are the biggest bitch that ever lived, you know that?
NANNY. All I've ever wanted is for us to survive, Louise. If that makes me a bitch, then I guess I'm a bitch. *(Louise and Nanny sit in silence. As Louise pours herself another drink, we see Jody approaching the door. He knocks.)*
JODY. *(Through door.)* Lou? It's me.

NANNY. *(Referring to Jody.)* That's all I need. *(Louise opens the door. Jody enters, dressed in a suit and tie.)*
LOUISE. *(Pleased to see him, but still shaky from the argument.)* Jody.
JODY. I knocked on your door down the hall … I hope I'm not intruding, or anything. *(Acknowledging Nanny.)* Mrs. White. *(Nanny nods curtly and sits on Murphy.)*
LOUISE. Don't be silly, it's always good to see you. Are you here to pick up Helen?
JODY. Well, we hadn't scheduled anything today, but I thought I'd surprise her for a soda.
NANNY. She's in school, Jody.
JODY. I'm sorry … I guess I didn't realize … *(He hesitates, not quite knowing if he should stay or go.)*
LOUISE. No, no, it's good to see you, and Helen will be thrilled. *(Beat.)* Well then why don't you take a load off?
JODY. Thanks, Lou. *(He sits on the couch. Nanny's not too pleased at this unexpected visit.)*
LOUISE. You're so decked out. What's the occasion?
JODY. Oh, you know, "Dress like a success, be a success." The doc at Olive View said a man should always dress like he's going to work, even if he's not.
NANNY. What happened to that job you were supposed to get at the aircraft company?
JODY. Failed the physical again.
NANNY. I see.
JODY. I'm getting closer, though. In the meantime, I've always got the ol' coupon business. The ten cent commission on each coupon doesn't bring in a heck of a lot, but this way I can call my own hours while I get back in shape. Keeps me out of my mother's hair, too.
LOUISE. How is it, living with Nora?
JODY. Fine, pretty good as a matter of fact. She's got her real bad days, but she never complains. *(Louise shoots a subtle look at Nanny.)*
LOUISE. I know Helen gets a big kick out of spending time with the two of you. *(This isn't sitting well with Nanny.)*
JODY. Yes, well, my mama's pretty crazy about her little grandbaby, all right.
NANNY. If you two will excuse me … *(She exits into the bathroom, slamming the door.)*
JODY. Maybe I should go …
LOUISE. Just sit still. She just wants to be the center of Helen's universe. *(Nanny reopens the door.)*

NANNY. Listen, as long as the two of you are catching up, why don't you bring him up to date about the *new* "little grandbaby"! *(She slams the door again. Louise and Jody are silent for a beat.)*
LOUISE. *(Shaking her head, almost smiling.)* Damn her. *Damn* her. *(Jody sits silently.)* Oh ... what the hell does it matter anyway. It won't be long before the whole world knows. *(There is a slight pause.)*
JODY. Lou ... what about ...
LOUISE. Nick? *(She smiles ruefully and simply shakes her head.)* Wanna hear something funny? He called me ... his wife, Myrna, can't have children ... *(Pause.)* ... and he offered to adopt the baby. How about that? I mean, that's really funny, isn't it? Well, I told him what he could do with that idea ...
JODY. I'm sorry.
LOUISE. Don't be. I'm really happy about the baby.
JODY. Then I'm happy for you.
LOUISE. You're something, you know that? *(They hug. Jody rises to go.)*
JODY. Well ... I'll stop in another day ... give Helen a kiss for me. *(Louise nods. Jody reaches the door and pauses for a beat or two, thinking. He turns back to Louise.)* Lou ... if there's anything at all I can do ... I mean, what I'm trying to say is that if you want to, you can use my name on the birth certificate. I just want you to know that. *(He exits. Louise stands, silent, at the apartment door. Nanny slowly opens the bathroom door. Blackout.)*

Scene 8

Lights up on 102. Seven months later. Louise, hugely pregnant, is at the kitchen table. She has a short drink in her hand, the newspaper, and half a bottle in front of her. Helen enters excitedly.

HELEN. Nanny! Nanny!
LOUISE. *(Calls to Helen.)* She's at the dime store.
HELEN. Mama, guess what! I got first prize in the drawing contest at school!
LOUISE. *(Lousy mood.)* That's great, kid.

HELEN. Mrs. Anderson says I'm almost good enough to work for Walt Disney, some day! Yessireebob, and then we'll all be on easy street!
LOUISE. That'll be swell.
HELEN. What's wrong? *(Louise hands Helen the newspaper. Reading aloud.)* The contest winner for "Name Trigger's Son" is Mr. Alan Brown of Riverside. Mr. Brown sent in the winning entry, "Trigger Jr." Oh, Mama …
LOUISE. Trigger Jr. Trigger … fucking … Junior. Stupid. Any idiot could've come up with a crappy name like that! It's fixed. The whole goddam world is fixed! Trigger Jr. Christ. *(Louise takes a swig.)*
HELEN. Mama…?
LOUISE. I'll tell you something, baby. This world is not kind to people like us. They hate originals. But hey, if you're just your average run-of-the-mill "Joe," it's "Well helloooo there! Come right in! Be our guest!" An' you wanna know why? I'll tell you why. Because being just plain ol' run-of-the-mill makes all the ordinary people feel safe. You got that?
HELEN. Yes. *(Frightened.)*
LOUISE. *(Pacing.)* And Hollywood is the worst! Not an original thought in the whole goddam town! "Trigger Jr." You better be good and careful Walt doesn't turn around and screw you! *(Louise winces. She grabs her belly.)*
HELEN. Mama, are you okay?
LOUISE. I think the baby … I think … oh boy. *(Sits, wincing again.)* This may be it, Helen.
HELEN. *(Getting a pot off the stove.)* I'll boil some water! *(Louise heads for her coat and hat.)*
LOUISE. Baby, you see too many movies.
HELEN. Mama! What are you doing!? Lie down!
LOUISE. *(Smiles, stroking Helen's hair.)* I'll just get on the streetcar and go to the hospital. Don't worry, it's okay. I have plenty of time. You took fourteen hours.
HELEN. You shouldn't go alone!
LOUISE. When your Nanny comes home, you tell her where I am, okay? *(Helen nods. Louise stands there for a beat. She picks up the bottle, pours and drinks. Lights down as she is donning her coat and hat. Blackout.)*

Scene 9

Lights up on roof. Helen and Jody are entering the roof. Jody is slightly winded. Both are casually dressed.

HELEN. This is it, Daddy!
JODY. Wow, you can see all of Hollywood from here.
HELEN. Do you wanna sit down?
JODY. Maybe for a second. I'm afraid my lungs aren't what they used to be. I got tired just watching you run up and down the beach. You sure are fast, Punkin'.
HELEN. I might try out for the Olympics some day!
JODY. I bet you'd make it, too! Y'know, I ran track in high school.
HELEN. You did?
JODY. Yep. Was pretty fast myself. *(Remembering.)* I sure did love to run. *(Beat.)* All you kids play up here?
HELEN. Yeah. We play Tarzan, Sheena Queen of the Jungle, pirates ... Oh! And this is the best part. *(Helen pulls Jody over to an air shaft calling down into it.)* Hellooooo! See? Wanna try it?
JODY. Sure. *(Bends over the shaft.)* Hellooooo!
HELEN. *(We hear the echo. Jody coughs a little.)* This is *my* special place. I like to look up at the clouds and make out faces.
JODY. Well, let's just see what we can find up there. *(Beat.)* Oh! I see somebody!
HELEN. Where?
JODY. *(Points.)* See where the sun is peeking through those banks of clouds ... well ... just to the right ... see it?
HELEN. I'm not sure.
JODY. Now squint just a bit. It's a little baby's face. See those two puffy clouds? They're her fat little cheeks. She looks just like you when you were born!
HELEN. Was I fat?
JODY. You were just right. Perfect. *(Beat.)* Your baby sister, Alice ... she's a real little doll, isn't she, Punkin'?
HELEN. Mama says she's the most beautiful baby she ever saw. Nanny wasn't too thrilled at first, but as soon as she saw Alice, she fell in love with her too.

JODY. How is your mother?
HELEN. She has her good days. She hasn't gone out much since Alice was born. Says she's still "recuperating." *(Beat.)* But I think it's because she's blue.
JODY. Gotta be tough raising a little baby by yourself.
HELEN. I help her a lot, so does Nanny. Bill, too.
JODY. *(Beat, thoughtful.)* He's a good man, Bill.
HELEN. Yeah. *(Beat, making a face.)* I just don't like the diaper changing.
JODY. *(Laughs.)* I'll bet you're real good with her. Tell ya what, I'll try to come around a little more often, spend some time with her.
HELEN. *(Hopeful.)* Mama sure would like that, Daddy. Maybe you could get an apartment in the building?
JODY. Well, I don't think I could do that, Punk. *(Reading Helen's disappointment.)* You ever hear the expression "water under the bridge"? *(Helen nods.)* Well, that's me and your mother.
HELEN. What kind of water?
JODY. Muddy. The kind that you can never really clean up. Big mistakes that can't be taken back. *(Beat.)*
HELEN. Poor Alice.
JODY. Hey. I think she's awful darn lucky to have a big sister like you. Heck, before you know it, she'll soon be big enough to play up here with you, instead of her rattle.
HELEN. I'll teach her everything I know.
JODY. Like what?
HELEN. Well, like how to pretend to be a whole radio show.
JODY. You pretend to be a radio show?
HELEN. I even fool the neighbors!
JODY. Well, how about that.
HELEN. *(Demonstrating her radio show to Jody.)* "Welcome once again, ladies and gentlemen, to our show! Today's star of the week is Miss Jeanette MacDonald! Jeanette, may I say how lovely you look today?"
 (As Jeanette:) "Why, thank you, Jimmy."
 (As Jimmy:) "And are you going to sing us a little ditty today, Jeanette?"
 (As Jeanette.) "I'd be delighted to, Jimmy. This song may be familiar to a lot of you." *(Belting out.)*
　　WHEN I'M CALLING YOOOOOO
　　WILL YOU ANSWER TOOOOO?
MAN'S VOICE. *(From somewhere in the building.)* TURN THAT

GODDAM THING OFF! *(Helen is pleased as punch. Jody laughs and applauds.)*
JODY. Why, that's just terrific, Punkin'! You sure fooled 'em all right! *(Jody begins to cough and then stifles it.)*
HELEN. We're putting on *The Wizard of Oz* in school, and I'm thinking about trying out for it.
JODY. Hey! You can be anything in the world you want to be. And don't you take no for an answer.
HELEN. Can I come stay with you again next Saturday?
JODY. Of course you can. Your Grandma Nora loves having you. It's fun for her to cook for more than just me.
HELEN. *(Still hugging, teasing him.)* Boy, Daddy, you may have to slow down on Grandma Nora's cooking. You're getting downright chubby!
JODY. *(Laughing.)* I haven't had a drink in ten months, and I had forgotten how good food tastes! You just keep praying for me like you do, and I'll never take another drop.
HELEN. *(Pulling apart, looking at him adoringly.)* I do, Daddy, I pray for you all the time.
JODY. Well, see? It works! Thanks for showing me your special place, Punkin'.
HELEN. Daddy.
JODY. Yes?
HELEN. Don't tell Nanny or Mama I brought you up here, okay?
JODY. Don't you worry, honey. This will always be between you and me. *(Standing side by side, holding hands at the edge of the roof, Jody looks out over Hollywood. Deep inhale — looking out.)* The view sure is beautiful up here.
HELEN. *(Deep inhale — looking at Jody.)* It sure is, Daddy. *(Blackout.)*

Scene 10

Lights up (dim). Apartment 102. One month later. We see Louise, Nanny, Dixie and Malcolm installing extra telephones. Racing forms are being taped on the cabinet doors. The baby, Alice, is on Murphy surrounded by pillows. Over this action we hear:

NANNY. *(V.O.)* Just how're we gonna manage any more, Louise, tell me that.
LOUISE. *(V.O.)* You think it's easy paying for two apartments? I begged you to stay in Texas a little while longer.
NANNY. *(V.O.)* What, until Helen turned forty?
LOUISE. *(V.O.)* Well, I'm sure as hell not gonna ask Dixie for any more handouts.
NANNY. *(V.O.)* You got another solution?
LOUISE. *(V.O.)* Mama, I'm doing the best I can.
NANNY. *(V.O.)* Well it's pretty obvious it's not enough. The welfare check runs out before the end of the month … this morning I sent Helen to school with a mayonnaise sandwich for lunch. We can't go on like this, Louise. We've gotta come up with *something!*
LOUISE. *(V.O.)* I know. I know. Just let me *think* will you? *(Lights all the way up — 102. They have set up a "bookie joint" in the apartment. There is a flurry of activity. There are papers taped to the inside of the kitchen cabinets that contain racing information. Louise, Dixie and Malcolm are all answering the four constantly ringing phones. They run from one to another as they ring. Helen enters in a hair net and curlers and puts her head in the oven to dry her hair. Nanny is writing down the bets as they come in. There's lots of noise, activity. The dialogue overlaps, and everyone is at a high pitch. Note: Think "newsroom" in* The Front Page.*)*
RADIO ANNOUNCER. "And they're off! And it's Louisiana Delta leading by a length over Hushabye Baby. Hushabye making a dash on the outside. And it's Shamrock Shimmy passing Five Star General for the third position. Louisiana Delta still in front by a nose. Hushabye Baby pushing the lead. This will be a photo finish, Ladies and Gentlemen. Five Star General takes back third. It's

Louisiana Delta in a dead heat. Hushabye Baby moving past the leader by a head, by half a length — incredible! It's Hushabye Baby to win. Louisiana Delta to place. Five Star General to show."
LOUISE. Hello. Yes, got it Leroy. *(To Nanny.)* Mama … three and a quarter to win, on Stoker in the Fifth, for Leroy Klinker. *(Phone rings. Louise goes over to Alice, to turn her over. Malcolm picks up his phone and overlaps Nanny's dialogue.)*
MALCOLM. Yeah?
NANNY. *(Writing it down.)* "Three and a quarter on Stoker in the Fifth."
MALCOLM. Right. *(To Nanny.)* One lonely smacker, to place on Little Ham in the Seventh, for Max Fish. *(Phone rings. Dixie runs for it.)*
NANNY. *(To herself, writing.)* " … Little Ham … "
DIXIE. Yeah, hello. Oh, hi there!
NANNY. … Max Fish …
DIXIE. Of course, sweetie. Bye bye. Hey, Mae! Two-fifty to show, on Midnight Fig in the Sixth for Fannie Stone. *(Nanny writes furiously. Phone rings again.)*
LOUISE. Hello? Ragged Rascal in the Fourth, to win. Two dollars. *(Hanging up, to Nanny.)* Barney Davis. *(Phone rings. Malcolm grabs it.)*
MALCOLM. Y'ello!
NANNY. " … Barney Davis … "
MALCOLM. *(Yells to Nanny.)* Four bucks on Candy Apple Red in the fifth! Thank you, Jack, and my best to the Missus. *(He hangs up.)*
NANNY. Jack? Jack, who? *(Malcolm hits his forehead with his hand. [Oops!])* Oh for godsakes, Malcolm! Is there anything at all between those ears of yours? *(Phone rings again. Both Malcolm and Dixie dive for it. Malcolm gets it first, but Dixie takes it away from him.)*
MALCOLM. Hey! I got it first! Give it back!
DIXIE. *(To the caller.)* Yeah? *(To Nanny.)* Put a fin to place, on Fancy Dan for Sam Noonan. *(To Malcolm.)* You're not screwin' up anymore, mister. *(Phone rings again. Louise heads for it.)*
MALCOLM. That's not fair. *(He slumps over to Murphy, where Alice is. He is making "goo-goo, gaa-gaa" sounds at Alice.)*
LOUISE. Malcolm, please don't talk baby talk to her.
MALCOLM. What would you prefer? Spanish? *(Louise checks the baby. She's wet.)*
LOUISE. Helen! Cover for me, will you? I'm gonna change the baby. *(Louise takes the baby into the bathroom. Two phones begin

ringing at once. Dixie goes for one. She stops Malcolm in his tracks.)
DIXIE. Don't even think about it ... *(On the phone.)* Yeah? *(The other phone is still ringing.)*
LOUISE. *(Louder.)* Helen! *(Helen's head emerges from the oven in a hair net with pre-set curlers. She keeps them on for the remainder of the scene.)*
DIXIE. *(Hanging up, to Nanny.)* Two bucks on Mama's Boy, to show in the Fifth, for Casey Reese. *(Helen picks up the [still] ringing phone.)*
HELEN. *(Hangs up, to Nanny.)* Three smackers to win on Harry's Heartbreak in the Seventh, for Lucille Carlin. *(Louise reenters and places Alice back on Murphy.)*
LOUISE. Malcolm's gotta run those bets over to Bernard now, Dix, or we'll be late on the last four races.
NANNY. You're gonna *trust* him to do that?
DIXIE. Don't worry, Mae, I'll be with him. *(Nanny shoots a look to heaven.)*
MALCOLM. What for? I can do it by myself!
DIXIE. C'mon, get movin'.
MALCOLM. Aw. For pete's sake. How come I always get the short end of the stick? This whole thing stinks, y'know that? *(Malcolm and Dixie exit.)*
NANNY. That boy is headed straight for the post office wall. *(As Dixie and Malcolm cross downstage, they run into two cops in the hall, making their way to the door.)*
COP #1. Louise Melton?
DIXIE. Uh ... no officer.
COP #1. Is she in there?
DIXIE. Gosh, I'm not sure ... they might still be in church ... *(Dixie motions to Malcolm to get to the door before the cops. He runs into 102 and locks it. The cops follow and knock at the door.)*
COP #1. Open up, it's the police! *(Louise, Helen and Nanny freeze.)*
NANNY. Jesus, Mary, Joseph!
LOUISE. *(Overlapping.)* Omigod, Helen! Mama! Quick! *(They all frantically scramble about in the kitchen, bumping into each other, grabbing the incriminating evidence off the table and hiding it anywhere they can ... under the cushions on the sofa, in the kitchen cabinets, under Murphy, etc.)*
COP #1. We said, open up.
LOUISE. *(Calling out.)* Just a minute! We'll be right there! *(She motions for Nanny to lie down on Murphy. Nanny shoves some paper-*

work under the pillow as she gets on the bed. Louise, heading for the door, looks around, sees the extra phone, grabs it tosses it to Helen who shoves it into the stove. Louise opens the door. Two cops enter 102. Note: The following action should be played "straight." Avoid being too broad. In other words, don't treat it as a comedy "sketch.") What is it, officer? (The cops begin searching.)
COP #1. We understand you're running a bookie joint here.
LOUISE. Who … me? Us? (The radio is blasting out a horse race. Helen turns it off abruptly.)
NANNY. (Lifting her head off the pillow.) Louise, is someone here?
LOUISE. It's all right, darling, try to rest. There's been some mistake, that's all. (Cop #2 opens the cabinets in the kitchen.)
COP #2. Looks like we got a winner.
COP #1. Okay lady, any other phones?
LOUISE. Malcolm. (They're caught. Malcolm goes to the stove, pulls out the phone and hands it over.)
COP #1. Got any money here from the bookie?
LOUISE. No! No! We never deal with the money, officer, please. As you can see we don't have much, and we were only doing this so I could feed my two baby girls and my poor, old, sick mother! (Nanny moans from her "sick bed." Louise rushes to her side.) Mama … Mama … are you all right?
NANNY. It's my heart, Louise. (Nanny feigns passing out.)
LOUISE. Omigod! Mama, Mama, please say something.
NANNY. (Opening her eyes.) I just feel so weak, I can hardly … (She sees the officers and screams.) Who are these strangers? What do they want? (She moans. Louise cries.)
COP #1. Okay, okay, just calm down, ladies …
LOUISE. All we do is take calls from customers and pass on the information to Bernard. That's all, honest! We don't handle any money. We don't even see Bernard.
NANNY. (Calling from Murphy.) I've never seen Bernard … Oh, baby, my pills! (Helen rushes into the bathroom. We hear meds crashing in the sink.)
LOUISE. Never. Hear that? We are small fry in this operation, sir. Really we are.
NANNY. (From Murphy.) Don't even know what he looks like.
LOUISE. We were just trying to make ends meet, officer.
NANNY. (From Murphy.) Though I hear he's quite petite for a man … but I wouldn't know, first hand. (Coughing.) Louise, did someone dim the lights in here?! (Helen rushes in with the pills.)

LOUISE. I'm here, Mama. I'm here. Oh, God, please …
HELEN. Am I too late? *(There is a pause. No one speaks. Nanny belches loudly.)*
LOUISE. Get thee behind her, Satan!
HELEN. Let all the evil come out. *(There is another slight pause. Nanny lets one rip. She fans the covers.)*
NANNY. Thank you, Lord.
COP #1. Okay, okay. We're leaving. *(On Louise's signal, Helen holds the door open.)*
COP #2. *(On his way out, to Louise.)* Just don't get involved in any activity like this again, Ma'am.
LOUISE. Oh NO! We've learned our lesson, officer. Thank you so much for your understanding. *(The cops leave.)*
HELEN. Yes, thank you for your understanding. *(Helen exits, following them into the hall. Nanny grabs her bottle of sherry, takes a swig and hands it to Louise, who also pulls on it.)*
NANNY. Oh dear sweet God in heaven … I thought it was curtains.
LOUISE. *(Begins laughing.)* Your face …
NANNY. Mine? You should have seen yours! *(Imitating Louise.)* "Oh NO! We've learned our lesson, officer. "
LOUISE. *(Doing Nanny.)* "I've never seen Bernard … don't even know what he looks like." However, I hear he's short as a duck. *(Laughing very hard. Nanny begins laughing.)* Petite!? *Petite!?* Christ, Mama!
NANNY. Well, he IS! It's the only way to describe him. Must be a glandular thing. *(Nanny and Louise are hysterical at this point. Their laughter peters out. The realization has hit them that this didn't work out very well. There is a pause. Each woman is silent in her own thoughts. Finally, Louise speaks.)*
LOUISE. At least it was going pretty good there, for a while … *(They stare into space.)*
NANNY. Got any more harebrained schemes? *(The lights dim slowly. Blackout.)*

Scene 11

Lights up — 102. Later that week. We see Jody leaning against the door. He's drunk, weaving unsteadily on his feet. He's in his suit, with a black armband. He knocks. Helen, coming home from school, walks down the hallway and sees her father.

HELEN. Daddy…?
JODY. Just one 'lil beer, Punk. That's all I had. She's gone to heaven … your Grandma Nora's gone … in the ground. *(Helen looks very worried. Choosing his words carefully.)* Just needed to steady my nerves, y'know? I miss her.
HELEN. I miss her too, Daddy. *(Beat.)* Why don't you come in and sit down? You just need to sit down. *(She helps him over to the couch. He teeters on the edge.)* You rest for a minute, I'll whip up some coffee for you. *(Helen goes into the kitchen and frantically looks for coffee and a clean cup in the messy kitchen. Calling from the kitchen.)* That's all you need. A good ol' cup of coffee! *(Helen has found the percolator, turned on the tap to fill the coffee pot. As she's frantically throwing the coffee into the pot and putting it on the stove, Jody slowly slides off the couch, winding up on the floor. Helen calls to him from the kitchen.)* Hey, Daddy! I got the part in the play at school! Isn't that wonderful? I'm nervous to do it in front of an audience, but Mrs. McNeil says that even the most seasoned professional … *(Helen turns around and sees Jody passed out cold.)* Daddy? *(Helen, alarmed, bends down and touches her father.)* Daddy? Are you all right? *(Jody moans, Helen begins to shake him.)* Wake up. Please, Daddy, please be all right. Wake up! *(She starts to cry and shakes him harder.)* Don't do this! Wake up! Please! Don't do this! Daddy!
JODY. *(Almost inaudible, waving her off.)* Go 'way …
HELEN. Look at me! Look at me! Wake up! Don't do this! *(Helen, hysterical, screams in his face. He mumbles something again, tries to sit up and falls back down.)*
JODY. … well, shit …
HELEN. I prayed for you, just like you said! Wake up! I prayed for you! I prayed for you! Wake up! *(Helen is screaming down at him at the top of her lungs, crying her heart out. Dixie and Malcolm running in.)*

DIXIE. Helen! What is it? What's wrong with you?
MALCOLM. What's she screamin' about?
HELEN. I hate you! I hate you! *(Malcolm sees Jody.)*
MALCOLM. Oh, brother! Get a gander of this. *(Dixie spots Jody, bends down and smells his breath. Helen is still crying.)*
DIXIE. Out like a light. C'mon Jody, let's get you up. *(Dixie tries to lift Jody.)* Malcolm, for godsakes, help me out here! *(They're unsuccessful. Helen runs to Murphy and curls up, crying into a pillow.)* Malcolm, run down the hall and get Louise. Hurry! *(To Helen.)* It's okay, honey. Your daddy's gonna be okay. Wake up, Jody, c'mon. Help us get you up. *(Louise and Malcolm enter.)*
LOUISE. Omigod. Jody, Jody!
DIXIE. Let's get him up on the couch. *(They finally get him up on the couch. Jody's conscious.)*
LOUISE. Malcolm, get me some water, would you? *(Malcolm brings Louise the glass of water, and she hands it to Jody. His hands shake as he tries to hold the glass, spilling the water.)* Aw, what'd you have to go and screw up for? Jody, can you try to stand up? *(Jody nods, weaving. He gets to his feet.)*
JODY. Oh brother … oh brother. My hat. I had a hat … *(Malcolm picks the hat up off the floor and hands it to Jody. Jody nods, takes it and puts it on his head. Trying to explain to everyone.)* Just one li'l beer, that's all … my Mama's gone. I'm sorry, Punkin' Kid … Lou. Ladies and gentlemen. *(He exits the apartment. Louise goes over to Helen to comfort her.)*
LOUISE. It's okay, baby, it's okay. Your daddy didn't mean it. Your daddy didn't mean it.
DIXIE. *(To Louise.)* You need any help?
LOUISE. Could you stay with Alice in my place for a while? *(Dixie nods.)* Thanks, Dix. *(As Dixie and Malcolm start to exit, Nanny enters, carrying a shopping bag. Nanny is oblivious to what she has walked in on.)*
NANNY. Thank God I made it home! You wouldn't believe the crowds at Penney's year-end sale. People pushing and shoving … rude, I tell you, pure-de rude! But I got the very last pair of drawers and socks they had. Two for the price of one! *(She stops and surveys the scene.)* What's going on?
LOUISE. Nothing, Mama. It's okay.
NANNY. I'm not blind, Louise. What's going on? What's wrong with Helen? What is it, sweetheart? Tell Nanny.
HELEN. … Daddy …

NANNY. What about him? *(Helen sobs.)* Well for godsakes, will somebody tell me what the hell is going on?
MALCOLM.   He was three sheets to the wind! *(Dixie cuffs Malcolm. They head for the door.)*
DIXIE. You keep your mouth shut, mister. It's none of your business. *(As they exit.)*
MALCOLM.   Now what'd I do? *(Helen has calmed down. There is a pause.)*
NANNY. That's it, Louise. No more visits with Jody.
LOUISE. Mama, he just needs ...
NANNY. HE needs? What about Helen? What about what SHE needs?
LOUISE. I know, I know ... you're right.
NANNY. Damn right I'm right.
LOUISE. *(Stroking Helen's head.)* Everything'll be okay, baby. Your daddy didn't know what he was doing.
NANNY. He knows damn well not to show up here drunk.
LOUISE. *(Still to Helen.)* Hey, why don't we all get cleaned up and go get a soda on the boulevard, okay? *(Helen nods.)* Here, baby ... feel better?
HELEN. Uh-huh. *(Louise hugs Helen.)*
LOUISE. I love you, baby.
HELEN. I love you too, Mama. *(Quietly.)* I got the part in the play.
LOUISE. You did? That's fantastic! *(Hugging her again.)*
NANNY. They don't make you pay for the costumes, do they?
HELEN. No. But maybe you could help me whip one up?
NANNY. Well, her costume isn't so tough to duplicate. I think I've got plenty of material around here. Where the heck are we gonna come up with some red shoes?
HELEN. No, Nanny, I don't need red shoes. Ilomay's playing Dorothy.
NANNY. Ilomay! Ilomay's too fat for Dorothy.
HELEN. Mrs. McNeil gave me the Good Witch.
NANNY. Louise, call the principal! That woman should be fired!
HELEN. No! Nanny, Mama, please!
NANNY. Putting that tub of lard in the lead part! We should sue the school.
HELEN. Nanny! It's okay. Honest! It's not Ilomay's fault.
NANNY. Well, whose fault is it?
HELEN. Mine. I got scared.
NANNY. Of what?

HELEN. The tryouts! I opened my mouth ... and nothing came out ... *(Almost crying.)* I'm sorry ...
LOUISE. Oh baby, you've got nothing to be sorry about. You just got a case of the jitters that's all.
NANNY. Sure, it happens to the best. Next time you'll be fine. You'll see.
HELEN. No I won't.
NANNY. Yes, you *will*.
HELEN. No I ...
LOUISE. *(Chuckling.)* Don't argue with her, Helen. *(Nanny smiles and hugs Helen. There is a pause. Louise picks up the uke and begins strumming slowly.)*
 WHEN THE RED RED ROBIN
 COMES BOB BOB BOBBIN' ALONG
 ALONG
(Nanny joins in.)
LOUISE and NANNY.
 THERE'LL BE NO MORE SOBBIN'
 WHEN HE STARTS THROBBIN' HIS OLD SWEET SONG
(At this point in the song, Nanny gives Helen a gentle poke in the arm. Louise picks up the rhythm.)
NANNY. *(Singing to Helen. Helen starts to warm up. Louise sits on the arm of the couch. Helen is between them.)*
 WAKE UP!
LOUISE and NANNY. *(To Helen.)*
 WAKE UP
 YOU SLEEPY HEAD
 GET UP
 GET UP
 GET OUT OF BED!
LOUISE. *(Overlapping the song.)* C'mon, Helen, help us out here!
LOUISE and NANNY.
 CHEER UP *(Helen joins in.)*
LOUISE, NANNY and HELEN.
 CHEER UP
 THE SUN IS RED
 LIVE, LOVE, LAUGH AND BE HAPPY.
(Blackout. In the dark: Malcolm and Helen singing:)
BOTH.
 WE'RE OFF TO SEE THE WIZARD
 THE WONDERFUL WIZARD OF OZ

WE HEAR HE IS A WHIZ OF A WIZ
IF EVER A WIZ THERE WAS
IF EVER OH EVER A WHIZ THERE WAS
THE WIZARD OF OZ
IS ONE BECAUSE
BECAUSE BECAUSE
BECAUSE
BECAUSE!"

Scene 12

Lights up on the lobby. A few weeks later, after the play. Malcolm and Helen are arm in arm, doing the same skipping step from the movie. Helen has on her Good Witch costume, and Malcolm is dressed as the Scarecrow. Dixie is at the desk, putting stamps on mail.

MALCOLM. *(Continuing to sing as Helen laughs.)*
BECAUSE OF THE WONDERFUL THINGS HE DOES!
DIXIE. How did closing night go tonight?
MALCOLM. *(Laughing hysterically, indicating 102 and down the hall.)* Oh, Mom, I wish all of you had been there tonight instead of last night!
DIXIE. How come?
MALCOLM. Everything went wrong! The Cowardly Lion's tail got caught under the Wicked Witch's house, the Wizard had laryngitis and sounded like one of the Munchkins.
HELEN. *(Interrupting.)* Nanny and Mama would have howled! When the Tin Man fell down and couldn't get up, I thought I was gonna pee in my pants! *(Malcolm becomes the Tin Man.)*
MALCOLM. *(Sings.)*
IF I ONLY HAD A HEART …
(He demonstrates with a stupendous trip and fall with accompanying sound effects. Helen can't stop laughing.) And the best part was when Mrs. McNeil shouted "Curtain! Curtain!" Just when Bobby was almost on his feet, it crashed down on his head! *(He demonstrates again. Helen joins him in making the sound effects. "Bang! Crash!"*

They laugh hysterically. Dixie laughs at their antics, enjoying their enthusiasm. Louise has stumbled out into the hallway from her apartment. She's out of her mind drunk, wearing a slip and her untied robe, holding a highball glass. Her hair is unkempt and stringy. She stands there swaying. Malcolm and Helen stop dead in their tracks.)
LOUISE. *(Quiet and deadly.)* What's going on out here? *(Bill enters from Louise's apartment.)*
DIXIE. Lou ... *(Louise ignores Dixie and bores down on Helen. Malcolm begins to back away. Helen is frozen.)*
LOUISE. Where the hell have you been?
HELEN. Mama ...
LOUISE. I've been lookin' all over for you, kiddo. What've you been up to? No good? *(Frightened, Helen doesn't respond.)* Answer me! Goddammit! *(Louise explodes. Louise slaps Helen across the face. Helen runs down the hall.)* Come back here! Don't you run away from me like that!
DIXIE. Jesus Christ, Louise!
BILL. Lou! *(Louise ignores Bill and Dixie, notices Malcolm standing there staring at her. As she pulls her robe together ...)*
LOUISE. Well, what are you lookin' at ... "Straw Man"? *(Louise moves toward Malcolm, who runs down the hall where Helen has disappeared.)*
DIXIE. Goddammit, Louise! That's it. *(She moves toward Louise as if to attack her. Bill gets in between them, reaching for Louise, trying to guide her back to her apartment.)*
BILL. I got it, Dixie ...
LOUISE. Don't you start trying to run my life, too. *(She wheels away from him, spilling most of the booze she's got in her glass onto her clothes.)* Great, great. Now look what you've done!
DIXIE. You'd better get her the hell out of here, Bill!
BILL. I got it.
LOUISE. You haven't got anything. *(Louise moves toward the door of 102, Bill follows her. Dixie exits. Lights dim on the hallway. Louise begins to open the door of 102. There is resistance from the other side.)* Mama. Mama! Goddammit, let me in. *(Lights up on 102. Nanny is standing against the door, hearing everything. She won't let Louise in. Louise presses up against the door, Nanny shoves harder and locks it. We've never seen the door locked before. Now yelling very loudly.)* LET ME IN, MAMA! Open the door NOW.
BILL. *(Trying to stop Louise.)* Louise, for godsakes, let's go back and get you cleaned up. You're soaking wet.

LOUISE. Shut up.
BILL. No, Lou. YOU shut up. *(She does, staring at him. He's never been hard on her before.)* You don't have the slightest clue as to what you just did, do you?
LOUISE. *(To door of 102, weaker.)* Open the door, Mama. Open … the … door … *(Nanny still won't let her in.)*
BILL. *(Relentless.)* You *hit* her, Louise. *(Louise begins to cry, leaning up against the door. Over all of this, we see Nanny reacting. Beat.)* Why, Lou? Why?
LOUISE. I don't know. I don't know … *(Bill holds her as she sobs.)*
BILL. Lou …
LOUISE. Oh … my baby, I'm so sorry. Goddammit … I wish I was dead.
BILL. *(Softening, but into her eyes, focused.)* Jesus, Lou. None of us has much in this world, but what we DO have is each other. *(Stroking her hair.)* Sshh, sshh, Louise … why won't you marry me? Please. Let me take care of you. Let me help you. I love you so much. *(Nanny reacts. Bill looks Louise in the eye. She's a mess, soaked clothes, mascara running, hair a mess, bloated.)*
LOUISE. Why?
BILL. Because you're the most beautiful girl I have ever known. You take my breath away, Louise. *(Beat, quietly.)* Marry me. *(Nanny is holding her breath.)*
LOUISE. *(Quiet, almost childlike.)* Yes.
BILL. Yes? *(See Nanny react … yes! She then slowly opens the door to 102, and quietly makes her way into the bathroom. Lights up on the roof, simultaneous. Helen and Malcolm are play-acting. They've taken off their Oz costumes and are in their regular clothes. The surrounding lights of Hollywood glow around them, giving this scene a magical feeling. They are fluid and carefree … beautiful. Malcolm is finishing up an imaginary sword fight, brandishing a stick.)*
MALCOLM. *(As Heathcliff.)* Take THAT, you villain! *(Malcolm "drags" his imaginary slain villain over to Helen's feet, bowing with tremendous flourish. The scene in 102 is continuing: Louise and Bill have entered 102. Nanny, for once, quietly observing. Obviously thrilled at this turn of events, she doesn't want to interrupt [and possibly ruin things].)*
BILL. Let's do it right away. Tonight.
LOUISE. *(Sniffling.)* I think you're nuts.
BILL. About you. We can go to Vegas.
LOUISE. Tonight? *(Beat.)* Okay … *(They hug. On the roof:)*

MALCOLM. My Queen, Catherine, he shall torture us no more! *(He and Helen do a child's version of a corny movie embrace.)*
HELEN. *(As Catherine.)* Oh, Heathcliff! You killed him! You killed the Black Knight!
MALCOLM. He deserved it for all his wicked deeds. *(In 102:)*
LOUISE. But I don't have a dress …
BILL. I'll buy you a dress. A blue dress, to match your eyes. *(On the roof:)*
HELEN. *(As Catherine.)* Oh! I love this castle! Let's never leave it! *(Helen twirls in a circle. The entire roof is now their "castle." In 102 apartment:)*
LOUISE. *(Fussing with herself.)* I'm a mess.
BILL. A beautiful mess. *(He takes her in his arms and kisses her, smoothing her hair.)* I'll take care of you, Lou. And Mae, and Helen, and Alice. I promise. *(Nanny's reaction. Lights dim on 102. On the roof:)*
HELEN. *(Helen runs to the edge, throwing her arms in the air:)* Oh, Heathcliff! Make the world stop here! *(Curtain.)*

End of Act One

ACT TWO

Scene 1

Lights up on 102. Ten years later. Nanny is snoring on Murphy. "Big Ben" ding-a-lings from the kitchen cabinet. Helen, covered over her head in a blanket on the couch, rises. She's now college age. Stumbling to the kitchen, she shuts off the alarm, leaving the cabinet door open.

NANNY. Helen! For godsakes, the ticking! *(Helen shuts the door to Big Ben and goes into the bathroom. Splashing water on her face, she begins to get dressed. Her clothes hang on the shower rack [there is no shower curtain].)*
HELEN. It's okay, Nanny. Go back to sleep. I'm going in early today. I'll be home late.
NANNY. Aren't you going with Alice and me to the movies tonight?
HELEN. I can't. I have to study for an exam after I get off work.
NANNY. I thought you were off today.
HELEN. One of the usherettes got sick, so I'm taking her afternoon shift. I can use the extra money for books.
NANNY. We could use that extra money for rent!
HELEN. Nanny, please don't start.
NANNY. ... wasting it all on UCLA.
HELEN. It's my money, Nanny ... I saved it.
NANNY. College is for rich people.
HELEN. And UCLA's for us poor ones. It's not that expensive, Nanny.
NANNY. *(To Helen.)* Excuse me, Missy, but from where I sit, FORTY-TWO DOLLARS for tuition is a fortune! More'n we pay for rent every month, and for what?
HELEN. Nanny, why do we have to go through this every morning?
NANNY. ... when you could take that money and enroll in Woodbury Secretarial School.

HELEN. I don't want to be a secretary!
NANNY. IT'S A REAL JOB! *(Alice enters. She's bordering on adolescence. She settles at the kitchen table, pulls out a bottle of nail polish from her bag and begins doing her nails.)*
HELEN. I have to go. *(To Alice.)* C'mon, Sissy, I'll walk you to the bus stop.
ALICE. I'm not going to school today. My hip hurts.
HELEN. *(Not again.)* Yesterday it was your toe.
ALICE. Well ... today it's my hip.
HELEN. Well ... maybe we should just skip the sixth grade and stick you in the old folks' home.
ALICE. It's true! I think I may be coming down with something. I'd better lay low for a while.
NANNY. *(To Alice.)* You can help me clip coupons.
HELEN. *(To Nanny.)* No! *(To Alice.)* Alice, get your books, you're going to school if I have to carry you in.
ALICE. *(To Nanny.)* Do I have to? *(Nanny shrugs her shoulders.)*
HELEN. Yes. *(To Alice.)*
ALICE. All right! All right! *(Faking a hurt hip as she gets up.)* I'll get my books. *(Alice exits.)*
HELEN. Nanny, you've got to stop letting her get away with that.
NANNY. *(Defensive.)* Why, in God's name, can't you come off this high horse of yours ...
HELEN. ... and why, in God's name, is wanting to make something of yourself being on your "high horse"? *(Beat.)*
NANNY. I swear, Helen, you're just like your mother.
HELEN. *(Quietly.)* No, I'm not. I'm not anything like Mama.
NANNY. I give up. *(She heads for the bathroom. Beat. Helen grabs her books. On her way out she calls to Nanny:)*
HELEN. Bye, Nanny ... I love you. *(She exits into the hallway. Lights out on 102. Lights up on hallway. Alice "limps" toward Helen, handing her a dollar.)*
ALICE. Here. Bill left us some money this morning. A buck apiece. I'm gonna go to Thrifty's. They have a new lipstick, "Congo Red."
HELEN. *After* school.
ALICE. *Yes,* after school. *(As they exit the building, we see Louise standing in the shadows, in her robe. Her hair is messy, and she looks awful. She moves effort-fully to 102 and opens the door.)*
LOUISE. Mama?
NANNY. *(From the bathroom.)* In here.
LOUISE. Lemme have one of your phenobarbitals, will you?

(*Blackout. In the dark, noise from 102: Dinner is being eaten. Sound of plates, knives, forks, etc.*)
LOUISE. *(V.O.)* So this guy comes home unexpectedly, see, an' he catches his wife in bed with another man … so the husband grabs him by the neck an' screams, "What the hell are you *doin'*?" An' the wife sits up and says to the strange man, "Didn't I *tell* ya he was stupid?" (*We hear Louise laughing loudly at her own joketelling, Bill is chuckling.*) I got another one …

Scene 2

Lights up on 102. Late that afternoon. Louise, Bill, Alice and Nanny are just finishing up dinner. Alice is reading a comic book at the table. Louise is drinking.

BILL. That was a good one, Lou. You sure can tell 'em …
LOUISE. Shut up. I got another one …
NANNY. I wish you'd quit it, Louise, and get on some other subject. *(Indicating Alice.)* There is a *child* present, remember … (*Alice rolls her eyes and shakes her head. Louise gets up and pours herself another one. Nanny is throwing the dishes in the sink.*) We can clean up later, after Nelson and Jeanette.
ALICE. I don't wanna see Nelson and Jeanette. Every time the Vogue has one of those old movies playing, we have to go. I HATE Nelson and Jeanette. *(Mimics Nelson.)* "ROSE MARIE, I LOOOVVVE YOU!" Ugh.
LOUISE. *(Laughs, takes a drink.)* I'm with you, kid. (*Louise pushes her full plate away.*)
NANNY. *(To Alice.)* Now don't you talk about my Nelson Eddy that way.
BILL. Lou, you didn't touch a bite. *(Louise waves him away.*) Please, eat a little something.
LOUISE. Do you mind? I just don't happen to be a fan of Mama's meatloaf. That okay with you? (*Bill gives up. Helen enters, sits on the couch, removes her shoes and begins to rub her feet.*)
ALICE. Oh goody, you're home. *You* can go to the movies with Nanny.

HELEN. I've *been* at the movies all day.
ALICE. You're so lucky. You get paid a whole sixty-five cents an hour to see Betty Grable! It's not fair!
HELEN. Right. Life's not fair. I'm rich and you're not. *(Goes to table.)* What's to eat?
ALICE. *(Holding up her plate.)* Nanny's meatloaf.
HELEN. Never mind. *(Louise guffaws, Helen and Alice stifle a smile. Nanny is not amused.)*
BILL. *(Coming to Nanny's defense.)* I like it.
NANNY. Thank you, Bill.
LOUISE. *(Finishing her drink.)* Then you can have mine. *(Louise goes into the kitchen to pour herself another one. Bill watches her. Noticing Bill.)* Will you quit lookin' at me like that?
NANNY. *(To Helen.)* I thought you were working late.
HELEN. That was the initial plan. *(Pause.)* The projector blew up.
NANNY. What?
HELEN. Boom.
ALICE. Wow.
NANNY. You still get paid for the night, don't you?
ALICE. What happened?
HELEN. *(Milking the moment.)* It was pretty incredible, if I do say so myself.
ALICE. What?
HELEN. *(Enjoying the teasing.)* Yep … pretty incredible.
NANNY. Helen, for heaven's sake!
HELEN. I have to set the scene …
LOUISE. *(Laughing.)* You sure as hell have a flare for the dramatic, baby.
HELEN. Well, here I am at my post in the lobby, see, and all of a sudden I hear the audience yelling at the screen. I go in … and … gasp! There's NO BETTY GRABLE! Nothing! Mr. Claypool, the manager, runs up on stage and announces to the crowd that everything will be okay, "Just give us a couple of minutes." Then he hightails it outta there and heads for the projection booth. A couple of minutes go by, and everybody starts throwing candy wrappers and stuff at the screen. Some are yelling for their money back. Next thing I know, Claypool orders *me* to get up there and calm 'em down! He pushes me down the aisle towards the stage, and heads back to the booth! So now I'm up there on the stage … all by myself.
ALICE. Are they throwing things at you?
HELEN. Nope, they're actually waiting to hear whatever it is *I'm*

gonna say …
ALICE. What'd you do?
HELEN. *(Pause.)* I turned into Danny Kaye.
NANNY. You what?
HELEN. Remember him in *Up in Arms*, Nanny? That scene where he was in the lobby of a movie theater, and all these people are waiting in line to get in? And to keep everybody happy, he acts out the movie for them?
NANNY. Omigod, you didn't!
HELEN. "Ladies and Gentlemen, while they're fixing the projector, I've been asked to fill you in on where we left off."
LOUISE. *(Taking a swig.)* Am I loving this, or what?
HELEN. The weird part is, even though a lot of them got up and left, there was a whole bunch who stayed put. *(Helen begins to "take the stage" and demonstrate. Quickly rattling off the plot to the "movie audience.")* As you recall, Ladies and Gentlemen, "Harry" played by handsome John Payne, was starring in a vaudeville show where he discovered "Honey," played by adorable Betty Grable, in the chorus. "Harry" put "Honey" in his vaudeville act, taught her everything he knew, and they became a big hit … and … *(Winks.)* they had also been shot by Cupid's arrow … everything up to this point was peachy keen … and *now* we come to the part you've missed … *(At this point, Helen begins to act out the scene, doing all the parts.)* We find ourselves in the backstage dressing room. Honey and Harry have just finished their act. Honey is alone. There's a knock on the door. *(Helen raps on the bathroom door.)*

(Helen as Honey:) "Come in."

(As herself:) And standing there is this distinguished looking man.

(As Man:) "Miss Honey, allow me to introduce myself. My name is … Florenz Ziegfeld."

(As Honey: in a dither.) "Ohhh, what an honor, Mr. Ziegfeld. Harry's not here, but please wait! Please sit down! He'll be back in a sec."

(As Ziegfeld: sitting.) "Actually, it's you I came to see."

(Helen jumps up and becomes Honey.) "Me?"

(Helen sits and becomes Ziegfeld.) "Yes, you. I enjoyed your performance tonight very much, and *(Rising.)* I'm here to offer you the lead in my next *Follies*."

(As Honey:) "Me?"

(As Ziegfeld:) "Yes, you."

(As Honey:) "Ohhh! Harry'll be so excited! We've always want-

ed to be in the *Follies!*"

(As Ziegfeld:) "I'm afraid the offer is for you, only."

(As Honey:) "But Harry and I are a team."

(As herself: whispering.) In the meantime, we see Harry out in the hall listening to all this. *(Helen demonstrates Harry's anguish, by putting her fist in her mouth, trying not to cry too loudly. Louise, Nanny, Bill and Alice laugh at Helen's antics. Even Nanny is amused.)*

(As Ziegfeld:) "I'm sorry, but there's no room for him."

(As Honey:) "Well, then *I'm* sorry, but there's no room for me, either."

(As Ziegfeld:) "Miss Honey, do you realize what you'll be giving up?"

(As Honey: on the verge of tears.) "I appreciate it, Mr. Ziegfeld, honest I do … but … no Harry, no me."

(As Ziegfeld:) "Very well. I wish you the best, Miss Honey."

(As herself:) Mr. Ziegfeld exits. Now here comes the big moment. Harry enters the dressing room.

(As Harry: looking down at Honey.) "Hey there, Honey."

(As Honey: looking up at Harry.) "Hey there, Harry."

(As Harry: looking down at Honey.) "Honey, I've been meaning to talk to you about something … "

(As Honey: looking up at Harry.) "What is it Harry?"

(As Harry: looking down at Honey.) "Well, I've been working on a sensational new act, see … "

(As Honey: looking up at Harry.) "Oh, Harry. That's great!"

(As Harry: looking away, lying through his teeth.) " … for *me*."

(As Honey: looking up at Harry.) "What do you mean?"

(As Harry: looking down at Honey.) "What I'm tryin' to tell ya is, it's a great opportunity for me, and there's just no room in it for you."

(As Honey: starts to cry, reaching up to "shake his shoulders.") "Harry, you can't mean that."

(As Harry: flinging her "hands from his shoulders") "Don't you get it? You'd just be holding me back! Now, get outta here!"

(As Honey: sobbing.) "Wait for me, Mr. Ziegfeld, I'm coming … " *(Helen as Honey makes a dramatic exit. Louise, Nanny, Bill and Alice applaud. Helen is enjoying herself to the hilt.)*

(As herself:) Next, we see a huge calendar on the screen … flipping its pages all by itself … the months are flying by … And *now* we fade to a crowded street on Broadway. It's snowing. We cut to a theater marquee: THE ZIEGFELD FOLLIES — OPENING TONIGHT! There are crowds and crowds of hotsy-totsy folks all

dressed up in the lobby. We hear the warning buzzer, and they all go in to take their seats. There's a long shot of a man's lonely figure. His collar's pulled up around his neck. He walks up to the box office.

(*As Harry:*) "I'd like the cheapest seat you've got."

(*As herself:*) Now we see ... it's *Harry!* (*Helen becomes the box office girl, chewing gum.*)

(*As Box Office Girl: Brooklyn accent.*) "Sorry, Mister. Yer outta luck. We're sold out. For the next four years."

(*As Harry:*) "*Ah please,* can't you help me? I've come such a long way ... I've just gotta get in."

(*As herself:*) The box office girl takes pity on him ... after all, he *is* pretty good lookin'.

(*As Box Office Girl: Brooklyn accent.*) "Well ... I got one left for standing room."

(*As Harry:*) "I'll take it!"

(*As herself:*) We cut to the stage, and up there surrounded by eight six-foot tall men in top hats, white ties, tails, holding canes ... is HONEY! The men are dancing and singing around her as she descends this huge marble staircase. (*Helen demonstrates.*) She's dressed all in white fur and chiffon ... she's beautiful. We cut to Harry, in standing room. He has tears in his eyes even as he smiles. The orchestra strikes up a different tune. It's "their song"! Honey starts to sing ...

ALICE. (*Sings.*)
  "ROSE MARIE ... I LOOOOVE YOOOOOOOOOOO.
NANNY. Shush, Alice! (*To Helen.*) Then what?
HELEN. Then I sang.
LOUISE. Then you what?
HELEN. (*Singing softly and slowly, acappela.*)
  I'M ALWAYS CHASING RAINBOWS
  WATCHING CLOUDS DRIFTING BY ...
LOUISE. (*Laughing and shaking her head.*) This is as far-fetched as the goddam movie!
HELEN. (*Singing softly.*)
  MY SCHEMES ARE JUST LIKE ALL MY DREAMS ...
ALICE. *Then* did they throw things?
NANNY. I coulda sworn that song was in another movie.
HELEN. (*Ignoring them, still singing softly.*)
  ENDING IN THE SKY ...
NANNY. (*Sings.*)
  SOME FELLAS LOOK AND FIND THE SUNSHINE ...

(Louise starts singing. They harmonize.)
LOUISE, NANNY and HELEN.
  I ALWAYS LOOK AND FIND THE RAIN
  SOME FELLAS MAKE A WINNING SOMETIME
  I NEVER EVEN MAKE A GAIN … *(As the song continues, Helen's voice becomes stronger, and we lose the voices of Nanny and Louise. The lights dim, leaving Helen in a spotlight all her own. Note: Instrumental music is introduced here. It's all in Helen's head. She is now singing out in full voice. Everyone else is still, and not looking at Helen. They are not aware of Helen's fantasy.)*
HELEN.
  BELIEVE ME
  I'M ALWAYS CHASING RAINBOWS
  WAITING TO FIND A LITTLE BLUE BIRD
(Modulating up.)
  HOPING TO FIND A LITTLE BLUE BIRD
(Modulating up.)
  WANTING TO FIND A LITTLE BLUE BIRD
  IN VAIN.
(The lights in 102 return to normal, and Louise, Nanny, Bill and Alice "come to life." There is silence for a beat.)
LOUISE. *(To Bill.)* Get me another one, wouldja? *(Bill takes the empty glass to the kitchen.)*
HELEN. They never did get the projector fixed. Everybody got their money back, and that's the end of my adventure. Ta da. *(Helen plops down on the bed.)*
NANNY. Wasn't that the one with Dan Dailey? *(Louise laughs harder. To Alice.)* Get your sweater. *(Bill is in the kitchen. He quietly puts the liquor bottle under the tap and begins watering down the booze. To Helen.)* Coming with us?
HELEN. Homework, Nanny. *(Louise spots Bill watering the booze.)*
LOUISE. *(Menacing.)* What are you doing?
BILL. *(Caught.)* Lou, I …
LOUISE. *(Grabs the bottle.)* Who the hell do you think you are?
BILL. I'm sorry, Lou. I just thought you'd had enough, that's all.
LOUISE. What are you, keeping score?
BILL. I didn't want you to get sick.
LOUISE. Since when did you become my "keeper"? *(Bill is silent. Helen, Nanny and Alice are very still. Louise looks at them.)* What're you all lookin' at?
NANNY. Louise, for godsakes …

LOUISE. *(To Nanny.)* And you shut up! It's all your fault anyway! *(To Bill.)* Kept harping on how you were our "meal ticket!"
NANNY. Louise, stop it!
BILL. *(Reaching for her.)* C'mon, Lou. Let's go. You need to sleep it off.
LOUISE. Not with you, that's for goddam sure! You know what you are? YOU ARE BORING.
BILL. *(Embarrassed in front of everyone.)* Lou, c'mon … please.
LOUISE. *(Waving him away.)* I said, LAY OFF! Go on, get outta here. I'm staying at Dixie's again tonight, anyway. At least *she* makes me laugh. I have *fun* with her.
BILL. We can have fun …
LOUISE. Now *that's* funny! NOW you're making me laugh. *(Louise pours a shot from the bottle, downs it, grimacing at the watered down booze.)* Mama, you got anything decent to drink around here?
NANNY. *(Angry.)* For godsakes, Louise, why don't you go home with Bill and sleep it off?
LOUISE. Home? With Bill? Now *you're* being funny, Mama! I haven't spent a night at "home" with Bill in … oh, I don't know … whassit been, Alice? A week, this time? *(This is news to Nanny and Helen, who exchange a look. Bill is utterly humiliated.)*
ALICE. *(Getting upset.)* Mama, let's go home.
NANNY. *(To Alice.)* Is this true? *(Alice nods.)*
ALICE. Please, Mama? *(To Louise.)*
NANNY. *(To Louise.)* What the hell is wrong with you?
LOUISE. Stay out of it, Mama. For *once,* just stay out of my life.
NANNY. *(To Alice.)* Why didn't you say anything to me about this? *(Alice can't answer. She's about to break down and cry. She runs to Helen, who puts her arms around her. To Helen.)* Did you know about this, too? *(Before Helen can answer, Louise interrupts.)*
LOUISE. Hell, Mama, it's no big deal. I've been campin' out at Dixie's for *ages* now. *(Bill just stands there, too embarrassed to be angry.)*
NANNY. *(To Alice.)* I can't believe you never told me about this!
LOUISE. Why would she? So you can stick your nose in where it doesn't belong?
NANNY. It's not right!
LOUISE. What's not "right" is you thinking that you can tell me what to do, where to sleep, and who to sleep with! Goddammit, Mama!
NANNY. Now, you listen to me Louise …
ALICE. *(Beginning to cry.)* Please, stop it, you two!

LOUISE. *(Barreling through.)* You don't get it, do you? It's not your choice, Mama, it's MINE. *(Gesturing to Bill and Alice.)* We're happy with this little arrangement, aren't we? Aren't we *all* happy?! *(Bill goes to the door. Not looking back, he quietly exits 102. There is a long pause as all four women look at the door. Blackout.)*

Scene 3

102 — later that night. The lights are out. We see Helen clearly in the bathroom, doing her homework by a single, dim light bulb. Bill appears in the hallway with two suitcases. He puts them down and scratches at the door quietly. Helen hears and goes to the door. He motions her into the hall. She closes the door behind her quietly. 102 is in darkness. Lights continue on Bill and Helen in the hallway.

HELEN. Bill.
BILL. *(Whispering.)* How is she?
HELEN. She's sleeping it off.
BILL. I just came to say goodbye, that's all.
HELEN. *(Pleading with him to stay.)* She didn't mean it, Bill. You know how she is when she gets that way …
BILL. *(Knowing better.)* I think this is for the best. *(Beat.)* Well… *(He reaches for his bags.)* Take good care of her?
HELEN. I will.
BILL. *(He kisses Helen, who hugs him.)* Please say goodbye to your Nanny and Alice for me. *(Helen nods, trying not to cry. Bill hands her some money.* Here, this'll help with some of the bills. *(He picks up his suitcases and starts to go. He turns back to Helen.)* You know, sometimes we did have fun. *(Bill exits, and lights dim on Helen watching him. Blackout.)*

Scene 4

Lights up on hallway. One week later. Nanny, Louise and Alice enter, cross downstage to 102. They're dressed up, made up. Louise is wobbly, but sober. She and Nanny are noticeably silent.

ALICE. How come we had to come home so soon? Why couldn't we go to the party after the show?
NANNY. Because you're too young to go to parties with a bunch of college kids.
ALICE. Well, I could've gone with you. You're old. *(Nanny shoots her a look. By now, they've reached the door to 102. They enter. Lights up on 102.)* That was soooo much fun! I'm gonna be like Sissy!
NANNY. I thought she was just gonna be in the chorus or something.
ALICE. *(Singing.)* "TAKE BACK YER MINK
TAKE BACK YER POILS
WHAT MADE YOU THINK
THAT I WAS ONE OF THOSE GOILS?
I'M SCREAMIN'! LA DAH DE-DAH … " *(Alice exits into the bathroom. Nanny and Louise sit.)*
NANNY. Why didn't she tell us? She's supposed to be majoring in English. *(Louise is quiet. They think about this.)* How come she never told us she switched her major a year ago?
LOUISE. Maybe she thought we'd disapprove.
NANNY. Well, I sure as hell do. *(Alice reenters, wearing makeup and some of Nanny's clothes.)* Now what're you doin' in my clothes?
ALICE. I have written a play, and I shall perform it for you now.
LOUISE. We've seen enough plays for one night. C'mon baby, let's cash it in.
ALICE. I wanna stay with Nanny and Sissy tonight.
LOUISE. Alice, please …
NANNY. It's all right, Louise.
ALICE. Yeah, I sleep with Nanny, and Sissy takes the couch.
LOUISE. Sounds cozy as hell. *(Louise exits. Lights out on 102 — lights up in the hallway. Helen enters the hallway. She's flushed with excitement, carrying a small bouquet of flowers.)*

HELEN. Mama!
LOUISE. Hey, there. Thought you'd be out all night whoopin' it up.
HELEN. I'm so sorry I missed seeing you after the show! It was like a bucket of worms backstage!
LOUISE. Yeah, it was somethin' all right. *(There's a slight pause.)* Well … 'night, kiddo. *(Louise starts down the hall.)*
HELEN. Mama … *(Louise stops, turns around.)* What is it, what's wrong?
LOUISE. How come you never told me you've been majoring in theater? *(Helen hesitates.)* Scared we'd piss on your dream?
HELEN. I just wanted to be ready for you to see me.
LOUISE. Well, you sure as hell were. You were the belle of the ball.
HELEN. Oh Mama …
LOUISE. Baby, do me a favor and lay off the modesty crap. So … you got plans?
HELEN. Tonight something just may have fallen in my lap.
LOUISE. Yeah?
HELEN. After the show, this wealthy looking couple came up to me and asked me what I wanted to do with my life. I told them I wanted to go to New York and maybe, someday, even be on Broadway, like Ethel Merman and Mary Martin … and the man gave me his card and said to call him next week.
LOUISE. Uh oh …
HELEN. No, no, not like that, Mama. His wife was there. He said he "may be able to help me"!
LOUISE. Well, nuttier things have happened.
HELEN. It's gonna happen. Am I crazy?
LOUISE. Sure you are. *(Louise turns and walks down the hall to her room.)*
HELEN. Mama … You looked so pretty tonight … Just like Joan Crawford, only better. *(Louise smiles, remembering that this is Helen's standard compliment to her.)*
LOUISE. Must be somethin', hearing all those people clap like that … *(Blackout.)*

Scene 5

Lights up on 102 — later that week. Helen is packing. Nanny is sullen. You can cut the tension with a knife. Helen finally breaks the silence.

HELEN. Aren't you going to wish me luck?
NANNY. Do you have any idea what we could have with all that money? *(No response. Helen resumes packing.)* Your mother says you're nuts, you know. She says you haven't got a snowball's chance in hell. She says this is all a pipe dream and you'd better come down to earth before it's too late!
HELEN. Nanny, why do you always put your words in Mama's mouth?
NANNY. I'm doing no such thing. *(Helen ignores this and continues packing. There is a pause.)* You'll be dead in a week. Your blood's too thin. *(Still no response from Helen.)* You're as crazy as she is. She was going to be a famous writer. She was going to interview Cary Grant. She was going to hit the jackpot … and where is she now? Lying in her bed down the hall, dead drunk, and pitiful as hell because she couldn't face the fact that she was ordinary!
HELEN. Is that what you think I am, Nanny? *(Pause. Nanny's silent. There is a knock at the door. Helen opens it. Jody is standing there, hat in hand, wearing a threadbare suit. He's carrying a brown paper bag. He's sober.)* Daddy …
JODY. Hey, Punkin' Kid. *(He enters 102.)*
HELEN. Daddy! I'm so glad you came!
JODY. Well, there's no way I wasn't gonna come by and wish you good luck on your trip. *(They hug.)*
NANNY. Well, I just wish you'd come by to talk some sense into her.
JODY. Hello, Mrs. White.
NANNY. I thought you were back in Olive View.
JODY. I am. I mean, I'm on my way. I've got an hour before the bus, and check-in time's any time before two o'clock … *(Chuckles.)* I'll probably get my same ol' cot … the docs there know me pretty well, by now.
NANNY. I'm sure they do. What's in the paper bag, Jody?

JODY. It's not what you think, Mrs. White. It's just a milk bottle. *(He pulls out an empty milk bottle.)* I'm supposed to spit into a bottle every time I cough, and give it to them when I get there, so they can analyze it. Once I'm clear for six months, I'll get sprung. *(To Helen.)* Your mama told me about that man who gave you all that money. That's really something.
NANNY. Wasting it on New York!
JODY. Well, I think it's swell. *(Nanny's about to shoot back at Jody …)*
HELEN. *(Interrupting just in time.)* Nanny, maybe you ought to check on Mama. *(Nanny's stung by this request, but manages to come up with some dignity.)*
NANNY. Well, fine. Seems that's all I ever do around here, anyway. *(As she exits.)* You two just go right ahead. *(She exits. There is an awkward pause.)*
JODY. You know, Punk, I haven't had a drink in almost three months …
HELEN. That's wonderful, Daddy.
JODY. … and I feel terrific.
HELEN. *(Lying.)* You look terrific, Daddy. Here, sit down. *(He sits at the kitchen table and begins to cough. He undoes the cap on the bottle and spits into it, keeping it hidden in the paper bag. It's a racking cough, and he's embarrassed.)*
JODY. Sorry. I guess that's not too attractive, is it?
HELEN. Let me get you some water. *(She goes to the kitchen, and pours a glass.)*
JODY. I'm just sorry I couldn't have seen you in your show. Your mama said you surprised the heck out of her.
HELEN. Yeah. That's what she said.
JODY. But I remember when you'd do your radio show on the roof for me.
HELEN. You were the only one I ever had the nerve to do that in front of. *(Helen returns with water and joins Jody at the table. Beat.)*
JODY. That man who gave you the money … gosh, he must have some swell job.
HELEN. He owns the building his office is in.
JODY. That's pretty successful all right.
HELEN. When he asked me how much it would take to get to New York and get settled, I didn't know what to say … so I just blurted out, "A thousand dollars," off the top of my head.
JODY. A thousand dollars …

HELEN. And before I knew it, he was writing me a check! *(Jody chuckles.)* Daddy, it was right out of *Magnificent Obsession*. He gave me these stipulations.
JODY. Like what?
HELEN. I'm never supposed to reveal his name. And if I make it, I have to promise to help others out like he helped me.
JODY. He sounds like a real nice man.
HELEN. He's a wonderful man, Daddy.
JODY. Yesireebob. *(Beat.)* So. What now, Punk?
HELEN. Well, I figure I'm going to give myself five years to make it, and if I'm not earning a theatrical living by then, well, I'll just come back home and try something else, like art. Teaching, maybe.
JODY. Well, it sounds as if you have your life all mapped out pretty good there. You know anybody in New York?
HELEN. No.
JODY. Never been further east than Texas …
HELEN. Yeah.
JODY. You scared?
HELEN. No. Yeah. A little.
JODY. Well, I hear New York's some swell place, and I'm sure you'll make lots of friends real fast. *(Nanny bursts in, upset, slamming the door.)*
NANNY. She's driving me crazy down there. I couldn't take it another minute!
JODY. What's wrong? Is Lou all right?
NANNY. What planet did you drop down from, Jody? She's a *drunk!* Surely you know what *that* is!
HELEN. Nanny!
NANNY. *(Whirling on Helen.)* How long do you think it'll last this time, huh? Soon as he gets "sprung" from that charity ward of his, he'll be out on the street inside of a week, with a real bottle in that paper bag!
HELEN. Please …
NANNY. *(Back to Jody.)* And you show up here out of the blue and have the nerve to tell her you think it's "swell" that she's taking that money and hightailing it out of here all the way to New York City, just because she was a "hit" in some piddly little college show … puffing her up, giving her false hope, making her think she can …
JODY. *(Exploding.)* Goddammit, Mae! She CAN! She can *do* anything she wants … *be* anybody she wants to be! Who made you God? Who gave you a crystal ball? Why is it you have to piss on

everybody's dreams? You did it to Lou, and now you're trying to do it to Helen! *(He begins to cough, hardly able to catch his breath. Helen tries to help him. Nanny gets some water and slams it down on the table in front of Jody.)*
NANNY. *(Relentless.)* Where's she going to live? Who's she going to trust? What makes you think there's somebody in that great big city who's going to give a damn! Who *has* ever given a damn about that child anyway?
HELEN. Stop. Please stop.
NANNY. *(Continuing.)* ... Louise? Who's now passed out down the hall ... who left her with me years ago, so she could become "somebody" in Hollywood? You? Where were you? And when you did show up, you were falling down drunk! *(She is crying now.)* Don't you dare tell me I'm pissing on anyone's dreams! *(Pause. Nanny turns to Helen.)* Who's going to love you? *(Jody's coughing has subsided and is replaced by his sudden remorse. He starts to exit.)*
JODY. Oh God help me. I'm so sorry. I'm so very sorry. I'm the sorriest sonofabitch I know. Forgive me. It wasn't supposed to be like this ... *(He is at the door and turns to Helen.)* It should've been me. I should've been the one ... to give you that money. *(Blackout.)*

Scene 6

Lights up 102. Months later. Nanny is reading a letter.

NANNY. "After the show we did at the Rehearsal Club, this agent came up and wanted to sign me! He's at William Morris, one of the best agencies in New York. They're going to send me up for a lot of stuff ... summer stock, Broadway, television ... this is a real break for me ... but don't worry, Nanny, I'm not counting my chickens. I'm still holding on to my job at Susan Palmer's Tea Room." *(Louise is on Murphy. She's not drunk, just feeling bad and out of it. Nanny sits on the side of the bed, reading Helen's letter.)*
NANNY. Well, I sure hope this agent's worth his salt. It's taken her long enough to get one. She oughta check up on this Morris character in *Variety* and see if he's on the up and up.
LOUISE. Mama, have you seen Alice? *(Alice is sitting at the kitchen*

table, plucking her eyebrows.)
ALICE. I'm right here.
LOUISE. Oh.
NANNY. How're you feeling?
LOUISE. Not so hot.
NANNY. You've got to eat something, Louise.
LOUISE. I need a drink.
NANNY. Only if you eat something.
LOUISE. I'd puke.
NANNY. I promise you won't.
LOUISE. I just wanna sleep.
NANNY. Just let me get some substance into you. *(Nanny gets a bottle of whiskey out of the kitchen cupboard and an egg from the refrigerator. She pours the whiskey into a glass and cracks the egg into it. To Alice.)* Nanny's little remedy. *(She returns, lifting Louise's head.)* Here, drink this, Louise … please, baby … for Mama. *(Nanny helps her down the concoction. Louise falls back on her pillow. The phone rings.)* Alice, get that. *(Alice ignores Nanny, plucking away.)* Alice? *(Nothing.)* Good Lord … *(Huffing, Nanny rises to get the phone.)* For cryin' out loud! You don't have any eyebrows left!
ALICE. They're my eyebrows, not yours.
NANNY. Well, I'm the one who has to look at 'em all day … and this is no time to be arguing about how ridiculous you look.
ALICE. You started it!
NANNY. Hello? Yes? Yes, operator, I'll accept the charges. *(Beat.)* Helen? Are you all right? *(Beat.)* Well, then why on God's green earth are you calling collect? What? Well of course I know who Ed Sullivan is! Where are you? What's going on? You waited so we'd be surprised? What? Tonight? What? You already did it? Yes, they're both here … Louise! What? Well, of course I'm surprised; dumbfounded's more like it. Well, of course we're gonna watch it!
ALICE. What is it? What's going on?
NANNY. *(To Alice.)* Hush up! *(Noticing the time.)* Oh, no! It's already on! Omigod! It's a quarter past eight out here! You're on in five minutes? How do you know? What? Right, okay, okay! G'bye! Get off the phone! I love you! G'bye! *(Hanging up.)* Alice! Louise! *(Nanny turns on the TV and begins adjusting the rabbit ears. Note: The TV faces upstage.)* She's on *Ed Sullivan* tonight! Louise, wake up!
ALICE. *(Excited.)* Ed Sullivan!
NANNY. Somebody got sick! Somebody couldn't do it, and they called her to come in at the last minute!

ALICE. Who got sick?
NANNY. How the hell should I know?
ALICE. It's already started!
NANNY. She said she's on in five minutes.
ALICE. How does she know that?
NANNY. She already did it! *(Nanny furiously moves the rabbit ears around, trying to get a picture. She's practically mangling them. Distraught.)* Dadgummed things!
ALICE. Here, let me do it! *(Alice wrestles with the rabbit ears, Nanny tries to shake Louise awake.)*
NANNY. Louise! Helen's on TV! Tonight! NOW! *(Louise mutters something incoherent.)*
ALICE. *(Calling to Nanny.)* I'm not getting anything! *(Nanny runs to the TV, she and Alice both wrestling with the rabbit ears, mangling them this way and that.)*
ALICE and NANNY. Oh! There! There's *Ed Sullivan*! *(We hear the music play and audience applause. Nanny looks over at Louise. Alice stares at the TV.)*
ALICE. Where's Sissy?
NANNY. *(She crosses to Murphy.)* Louise! Louise! *(We hear audience applause.)*
ED SULLIVAN'S VOICE. "And coming up next, we have young newcomer Helen Melton. Right after this word from our sponsor."
ALICE. Oh! She's next! Sissy's on next! *(The set goes on the blink! All "snow" and loud static. Alice begins to bang on it.)*
NANNY. Stop that! You'll break it! *(Shaking Louise.)* Louise … Louise … *(Shaking her harder, clapping her hands.)* Wake up! It's Helen! *(Louise stirs and mumbles. Nanny heaves her into an upright position. Alice turns up the volume. Louise opens her eyes. She's pretty out of it.)*
LOUISE. Is she home?
NANNY. No! She's on *Ed Sullivan*!
LOUISE. *(Trying to focus.)* No kidding … *(Louise tries to sit up. Dixie bursts into the apartment.)*
DIXIE. Lou! Helen's on *Sullivan*!
NANNY. We know! We know! Louise! *(Nanny shakes Louise awake. Alice is desperately trying to fix the TV.)*
DIXIE. What's wrong with the set?
NANNY. What does it look like, Dixie? DO SOMETHING!
DIXIE. It's the rabbit ears! *(Dixie starts fiddling with the antennae. Alice fiddles too.)* Alice, cut it out! You're screwing it up!

ALICE. *(Overlapping.)* Let me do it! I can do it! *(They get a fuzzy image. We hear laughter.)*
ALICE and NANNY. *(Overlapping.)* Ohhh! There she is! *(The picture clears. They freeze.)*
DIXIE. Shhh ... be careful! *Don't touch a thing!*
ED SULLIVAN'S VOICE. Next on the roster of our really big show is a young girl who hails from LA and who recently arrived in the Big Apple. Please give a big welcome to Miss Helen Melton. *(The three of them gingerly back away from the TV, trying not to disturb the picture. They gather around the screen and ... disaster! Loud static and snow. Louise is looking at the set from her perch on Murphy.)*
NANNY. Oh no!
ALICE. Shit!
DIXIE. Shit!
NANNY. Shit! *(Pandemonium! They all immediately jump up and begin trying to fix the rabbit ears again. Louise is making her way toward the TV set.)*
ALICE, NANNY and DIXIE. *(Overlapping.)* To the right! To the right!
NANNY. No, I tried it to the right!
DIXIE. Point 'em down!
ALICE. No! Down never works!
NANNY. Well, point 'em up ... oh Lord, please ... *(Alice, Dixie and Nanny continue to flay the rabbit ears, Louise hauls herself up off Murphy and moves the base of the rabbit ears ever so slightly. She then adjusts the rabbit ears so that they both point straight up. The picture comes back perfectly.)*
HELEN'S VOICE. *(As Man:)* "Miss Honey, allow me to introduce myself. My name is ... Florenz Ziegfeld." *(Louise sits back down. Nanny, Alice and Dixie stare at her.)*
LOUISE. You're blocking the TV ... *(The light of the television glows on their faces. Lights dim slowly on 102. Lights up downstage. We see Helen in travel clothes enter, carrying a suitcase, walking toward 102. We hear Helen's voice, doing her* Ed Sullivan *routine.)*
HELEN'S VOICE. *(As Man:)* "I'm here to offer you the lead in my next *Follies*."

(As Honey:) "Ohhh! Harry'll be so excited! We've always wanted to be in the *Follies*!"

(As Ziegfeld:) "I'm afraid the offer is for you, only."

(As Honey:) "But Harry and I are a team."

(As herself:) In the meantime, we see Harry out in the hall lis-

tening to all of this. *(We hear audience laughter.)*
(As Ziegfeld:) "I'm sorry, but there's no room for him."
(As Honey:) "Well, then *I'm* sorry, but there's no room for me, either."
(As Ziegfeld:) "Very well. I wish you the best, Miss Honey."
(As herself:) Now here comes the big moment. Harry enters the dressing room. *(Helen enters with her suitcases. She approaches the door of 102.)*
(As Honey:) "What is it Harry?"
(As Harry:) "I've been working on a sensational new act."
(As Honey:) "Oh, Harry. That's great."
(As Harry:) " … for me."
(As Honey:) "What do you mean?"
(As Harry:) "What I'm tryin' to tell ya is there's just no room in it for you."
(As Honey:) *(Starts to cry.)* "Harry, you can't mean that."
(As Harry:) "Don't you get it? You'd just be holding me back! Now, get outta here!"
(As Honey:) *(Sobbing.)* "Wait for me, Mr. Ziegfeld, I'm coming." *(Laughter and applause. Helen has reached 102.)*

Scene 7

She knocks on the door and tries the door knob. The door opens, and she enters. Lights out in the hallway.

HELEN. Nanny…? *(The room is in semi-darkness. Helen sets down the suitcase and reaches for a light. Nanny is lying on the bed, dressed.)*
NANNY. Helen!
HELEN. Nanny.
NANNY. Oh my God, you're here. You're home! *(Lowering her voice.)* I wasn't sure what time you were coming. Oh my sweet baby, you're home. *(They embrace. Helen reaches for the light again.)* No, don't. *(Almost whispering. Louise is passed out on the couch, covered with a quilt.)*
HELEN. What?
NANNY. Shhh … I want her to sleep it off. *(Whispering.)* She was

parading around the room the entire night, raving on about God knows what ... cussing a blue streak, drunk as a skunk. We thought she'd never pass out, dear God in heaven. She finally collapsed around seven this morning. Of course, I haven't been able to shut my eyes. This is one time I *wish* I could faint.
HELEN. Oh, Nanny.
NANNY. She hasn't been out since Jody died. *(Beat.)* I want you to know, Helen, I always liked your father.
HELEN. Why isn't she down the hall?
NANNY. She lives here now. And baby makes three. *(Off Helen's puzzled look.)* She was here all the time anyway. We couldn't afford the two places anymore. They just moved in a few days ago. I tell you, Helen, between her snoring and the booze on her breath, I'm about to die from sheer exhaustion and suffocation. You're too thin.
HELEN. I'm fine, Nanny.
NANNY. And it's all I can do to get your mother to eat. Once in a while, I get an egg down her ... and we can't even afford that anymore. *(Helen opens her pocketbook.)*
HELEN. Here, Nanny. *(Nanny looks at the money.)*
NANNY. I'll need more. *(Helen hands her more money.)*
HELEN. Where's Alice?
NANNY. One minute she's here, and the next thing I know, she's pulled a Houdini, hiding up on the roof. That child's running wild. *(Helen takes her coat to the hall, and brings her valise to the bed.)* Why can't you stay longer?
HELEN. Nanny, I wrote you.
NANNY. You've been gone a whole year.
HELEN. There are a couple of auditions coming up, and if I miss out on them, everything shuts down 'til after Christmas. *(Nanny sighs.)* But at least I got to come home for a *few* days!
NANNY. Why can't that agent of yours get you anything permanent?
HELEN. It takes time, Nanny.
NANNY. I'd get me a new agent if I were you.
HELEN. He got me that one shot on *Sullivan*, Nanny.
NANNY. Well then, if he's such a hot patootie, why hasn't he gotten you back on?
HELEN. I have to come up with some new material ... and that takes time.
NANNY. Where've I heard that one before? *(Nanny is heading out to the store. She refers to the roof.)* If you find Alice up there, maybe

you can talk some sense into her. *(Nanny exits. The lights come up on the roof. We see Alice. She is staring up at the clouds, quietly smoking a cigarette. She's wearing makeup, attempting to look older. Helen sticks her head out the window and softly calls up the air shaft.)*
HELEN. "When I'm calling you-o-o-o-o-o ... " *(Alice hears this and goes over to the shaft to call down.)*
ALICE. *(Excitedly.)* Sissy?
HELEN. Hi, Sweetie.
ALICE. You're home!
HELEN. Come on down here.
ALICE. No. It's better up here.
HELEN. Okay, wait a minute. *(Helen exits the bathroom by way of the shaft window and climbs up to the roof. During this action, Alice hastily throws away her cigarette, fanning the air with her hand. Helen arrives, and they embrace.)*
ALICE. Oh Sissy, when did you get here?
HELEN. A little while ago.
ALICE. Why *can't* you stay longer?
HELEN. Honey, I'm lucky I could afford this short trip.
ALICE. Nanny says you're rich since you were on *Ed Sullivan*.
HELEN. Not exactly. *(Helen looks around.)* God, I practically lived up here.
ALICE. Anything's better than down there. Now, when I get home from school, I have to sit in that damn dark room and wait for Mama to come to, so that just *maybe* I can turn on the TV ... *if* she's not too hung over. You're so lucky. *(Alice spots a lipstick on the floor.)* Ohh ... here it is! Thank God, I thought I'd lost it! *(She begins applying it to her mouth. Helen takes all of this in.)*
HELEN. How's school?
ALICE. *(Eyes to heaven.)* Ugh. Isn't this a great color? *(Blots her lips.)* There's a dance coming up. Mitch Perry wants to take me, but I'm thinking of asking Sammy DiLeo.
HELEN. Is he in your class?
ALICE. *(Laughs.)* God no! He's at Hollywood!
HELEN. Hollywood High?
ALICE. So?
HELEN. Nothing ... except why would he want to go to a junior high school dance? And a seventh grade dance, to boot.
ALICE. He wouldn't ... and that's why I'm not gonna ask him. We have a better time alone, anyway. *(Alice starts to leave.)*
HELEN. Where're you going?

ALICE. *(Pockets the lipstick.)* I'll be back at dinner time! I'm so glad you're here ... and don't worry, you can take Murphy with Nanny. I'll sleep in the tub. *(She hugs Helen one more time and exits the roof. Helen stares after her for a beat. Down below in 102, we hear Louise cough. As Helen is climbing back down the air shaft into the bathroom, the lights slowly come up in the living room . . just enough to see Louise on the couch. Helen walks into the darkened living room and purposefully locks the front door. Louise stirs. Helen approaches her mother.)*
HELEN. *(Gently nudging Louise.)* Mama ... Mama, it's me.
LOUISE. Hey. Helen. You're home.
HELEN. Well. Hi.
LOUISE. *(Louise pulls herself up.)* Help me up, honey. *(Helen props her up on the couch with a pillow behind her.)* Thanks, baby. What time is it? Never mind, it doesn't make much difference one way or the other. *(Louise is coughing. Helen brings her a glass of water.)* Lemme look at you. *(Helen turns on the light.)* Caught you on *Sullivan*. I was real proud, baby. *(Louise's deterioration is quite obvious. She's bloated and wheezes a lot between coughs. She's embarrassed about her appearance.)* Maybe soon, I'll be writing an interview with you, huh?
HELEN. *(Smiles.)* That'd be great.
LOUISE. *(Beat.)* You look good, kid. New York must be some swell place.
HELEN. Oh, yes. I love it ... I really do.
LOUISE. *(A long pause.)* I was with him when he died, baby. I'm tellin' ya, it was weird ... I was in my bed sound asleep, and out of the blue, I heard him calling to me "Lou, Lou." It was a goddammed vision, Helen. *(During this, she pours the glass of water into a small plant on the coffee table and then pours a drink into the empty glass. She slowly takes a swig.)* Well, I got up and I started phoning some of his buddies to try and track him down. He disappeared, y'know, after he got sprung from Olive View. The T.B. never really cleared up. Well, I hit pay dirt and found out he was in some dump in Venice Beach. I got there as fast as I could. *(She drinks to steady her nerves, closing her eyes and holding her breath, allowing the booze to burn her throat.)* He was dying. I stood there at the foot of his bed, and he stared at me for a while, and I said, "Jody, do you know who this is?" ... and he looked at me for a minute and said, "You were once my wife." *(Louise begins to cry. Helen tries to hold back her tears.)* He thought you were there, too, baby. He said to me, "Helen was here ... it's a shame, you just missed her. She came to see me."
HELEN. I didn't have the money, Mama.

LOUISE. The important thing is, he *believed* it. I sat on the bed holding his hand … the sun was coming up, and he died. Right then and there. Christ … life. *(They hold each other for a moment, and then separate.)*
HELEN. Mama. Let me have Alice.
LOUISE. What?
HELEN. Let me take her back with me to New York.
LOUISE. What do you mean? For how long?
HELEN. For keeps.
LOUISE. Why? I don't get it. What for?
HELEN. She's growing wild out here. It's too hard on Nanny, and you've been sick, and …
LOUISE. *(Frightened.)* No. No. Hey! How 'bout just for the holidays? She'd get a big kick outta that! Christmas in New York!
HELEN. I'll take good care of her.
LOUISE. How're you gonna be able to afford …
HELEN. I still have my part time job at the restaurant. And my agent's sure he can get me some extra work on TV, and then soon it'll be time to audition for summer stock. We'll manage, Mama. Don't worry. I'll *make* it work.
LOUISE. She's all I have left. I never had you … the old lady saw to that.
HELEN. Mama, please.
LOUISE. No.
HELEN. You've got to let me do this.
LOUISE. I said, NO! Goddammit! My whole life, everything I've ever loved has been ripped away from me, and I'm not gonna let that happen now! Why don't you just go back to your swell New York and do what you do, but leave us alone!
HELEN. You say you love Alice.
LOUISE. What the hell's that supposed to mean?
HELEN. *(Angry.)* You sit there and go on about how much you love her, when the only thing you really love is in that bottle! I'm not "ripping her away" from you, Mama, you did that all on your own a long time ago!
LOUISE. You shut your mouth!
HELEN. *(Overriding Louise.)* How long has it been since you were awake when she gets home from school, IF she's gone to school in the first place? You're passed out on the couch, and she either has to sit here in the dark with Nanny or hightail it out to God knows where, just to get away from all this for a few hours … and one of

these days she's not going to come back at all!
LOUISE. Oh God, oh God. *(Louise breaks down.)*
HELEN. *(More gently.)* Do this for Alice. *(There is a pause. Louise silently nods, coming to a realization, a clarity of thought, here. With a focus and intensity, she accepts the truth of the matter, and the fact that this will happen.)*
LOUISE. ... For keeps? *(Helen nods. Louise sits there for a moment.)* She'd never go with you if she thought it was for keeps.
HELEN. I'll tell her it's just for Christmas and New Year's.
LOUISE. When would you tell her the truth?
HELEN. After we're there a while ... maybe after Christmas.
LOUISE. Maybe she'll wanna come home?
HELEN. I'll convince her that it's best to stay with me.
LOUISE. She'll want to come home, you know ...
HELEN. We'll come home to see you and Nanny all the time! Just let her go for now ... please.
LOUISE. This is our secret. I'll tell the old lady later. She'd never keep this from the baby if she knew. *(They embrace. Nanny comes to the door, groceries in hand, and tries the knob.)*
NANNY. Louise! Don't lock this door! Open up! Are you all right? Let me in! Helen are you in there with her? *(Louise holds her finger up to her mouth to shush Helen.)*
LOUISE. Take real good care of her, honey.
NANNY. What's going on? Louise? Louise? *(Nanny keeps knocking and trying the doorknob.)*
HELEN. You know I will.
LOUISE. We're fine, Mama! Hold your horses!
NANNY. Louise! Open up this door!
LOUISE. Okay. Okay. *(Louise sends Helen to the bathroom.)*
NANNY. Keeping me standing in the hall, banging on my own door!
LOUISE. Quit doin' it then. *(Louise opens the door. Nanny enters.)*
NANNY. What's going on in here?
LOUISE. Nothing, Mama ... *(Blackout.)*

Scene 8

Lights up on 102 and the hallway. Alice is excitedly stacking suitcases outside the door to 102. She is dressed in her traveling suit.

NANNY. This'll be the worst Christmas yet, I just know it. Both of you gone.
ALICE. *(Calling back.)* It's only for three weeks, Nanny.
NANNY. Long enough. January seems like forever when you're alone. *(Helen is changing [in the bathroom] into her traveling outfit. Nanny is standing in the living room. Louise is sitting on the couch, in very bad shape. Alice reenters the apartment. Helen enters from the bathroom.)*
HELEN. We should go.
LOUISE. *(Struggling to get up from the couch.)* Let me walk you out.
NANNY. Don't bother, Louise. I'll go into the lobby with them. Why don't you just stay here?
LOUISE. I am perfectly able to walk them to the lobby, thank you very much. You always want to be the last one to say goodbye, the last one to get a kiss …
NANNY. That's not true.
LOUISE. Yes it is, Mama.
NANNY. No, it's not.
LOUISE. Yes, it is!
NANNY. All right, all right!
HELEN. *(Interrupting.)* We have to go now. *(They all walk into the lobby.)*
ALICE. We're gonna see snow, Nanny!
NANNY. You be careful, Alice. *(To Helen.)* Don't let her out of your sight. There are all sorts of cuckoo's running around New York.
HELEN. She'll be safe with me, I promise. *(Helen and Alice hug Louise and Nanny. To Louise.)* Thank you, Mama. I'll take good care of her.
LOUISE. I'll miss you both, baby. *(Alice goes to kiss Louise.)* Oh no you don't, you kiss your Nanny goodbye first.
NANNY. Louise, don't be ridiculous.

LOUISE. *(Deadly serious.)* I want to be last. This time. *(Nanny backs off. Alice kisses Nanny. Then Louise.)*
ALICE. I love you Mama.
LOUISE. I love you, baby.
HELEN. Please don't worry. We'll be fine. *(She kisses Nanny and Louise. Helen and Alice make their exit.)*
NANNY. *(Yelling.)* Helen!
HELEN. *(Offstage.)* I love you, Nanny! *(Nanny blows kisses and waves. She stands there for a long time, watching. She turns back to Louise, who is in the hall and watching her.)*
LOUISE. Mama, I'm sorry. About wanting the last kiss. I know how much it has always meant to you … it's just that …
NANNY. *(Interrupting.)* I know, Louise. I guess you had the right to do it this time. It's all right. *(Beat.)* She's going to stay there, isn't she? Alice. Helen's going to keep her…?
LOUISE. *(Nods.)* It's probably for the best. *(Nanny and Louise freeze. The young woman [Older Helen] reappears in her stylish dress with her fashionable eyeglasses perched on her head.)*
HELEN. *(Turning front into a small glow of light.)* Mama died four months later. Nanny lived to be eighty-one … and she's buried right next to Nelson Eddy. *(Lights fade on Older Helen. Nanny and Louise unfreeze.)*
NANNY. I just don't know how I'm going to live, Louise.
LOUISE. Honey, you'll outlive us all. How 'bout I whip us up some enchiladas, an' then we can listen to Kate Smith mooning that mountain … *(Arm in arm, they turn upstage. They take a few steps. They stop. Spotlight on the two women as we hear:)*
KATE SMITH. *(Singing.)*
>WHEN THE MOON COMES OVER THE MOUNTAIN
>EVERY BEAM BRINGS A DREAM, DEAR, OF YOU
>ONCE AGAIN WE STROLL 'NEATH THE MOUNTAIN
>THROUGH THAT ROSE COVERED VALLEY WE KNEW
>WHEN THE MOON COMES OVER THE MOUNTAIN
>I'M ALONE WITH MY MEMORIES OF YOU …

(Blackout.)

End of Play

PROPERTY LIST

Telephones, racing forms
Roller skates (LITTLE HELEN)
Movie magazine (DIXIE)
Suitcases (NANNY, HELEN, BILL, ALICE)
Drawing tablet and pencils (HELEN, JODY)
Teddy bear (LOUISE)
Tray of food: cheese, grater, enchiladas (LOUISE)
Purse (HELEN)
Medicine bottle (HELEN)
Glass of water (HELEN, MALCOLM, NANNY)
Big Ben clock (HELEN)
Cold cereal, bowl, sugar (HELEN)
Christian Science Monitor, string (NANNY)
Books (HELEN)
Mail (DIXIE)
Purse, money (LOUISE, HELEN)
Strapped schoolbooks (DIXIE)
Tea, cup (LOUISE)
Ukelele (LOUISE)
Opera glasses (MALCOLM)
Wet cloth (LOUISE)
Highball (LOUISE)
Purse with silverware, napkins, salt and pepper shakers (NANNY)
Bag with toilet paper rolls (HELEN)
Box of candy, bottle of sherry (LOUISE)
Dollar bill (JODY, ALICE)
Purse, coat (NANNY)
Bible (HELEN)
Bag with cosmetics (LOUISE)
Eyebrow pencil, leg makeup, mascara, etc. (LOUISE)
Purse (LOUISE)
Groceries (NANNY)
Newspaper, half bottle of booze (LOUISE)
Pot or kettle (HELEN)
Coat and hat (LOUISE)
Percolator, coffee (HELEN)
Black armband (JODY)
Hat (MALCOLM)
Penney's shopping bag (NANNY)

Postage stamps (DIXIE)
Stick (MALCOLM)
Nail polish (ALICE)
Comic book (ALICE)
Bouquet of flowers (HELEN)
Paper bag with empty milk bottle
Whiskey, egg concoction (NANNY)
Tweezers (ALICE)
Cigarette (ALICE)
Lipstick (ALICE)

SOUND EFFECTS

Screaming fans, cars, car horns
Alarm clock bell
Air raid sirens
Car honking
Ringing phones
Radio blasting horse race
Medicine crashing in sink
Sounds of eating
Instrumental music "I'm Always Chasing Rainbows"
Phone ring
Laughter and applause
"You'll Never Know Just How Much I Miss You"
"Taking a Chance on Love"
"Indian Love Song:"
"When the Red Red Robin … "
"Off to See the Wizard"
"If I Only Had a Heart"
"Rose Marie I Love You"
"I'm Always Chasing Rainbows"
"Take Back Your Mink"
"Ed Sullivan Theme Song"
"When the Moon Comes Over the Mountain"

MUSIC CUES

The following music cues and timings, which refer to the *Hollywood Arms* music CD, were used in the Broadway production of the play. The CD, which is required for all productions, is available from DPS. Cues #21 and #29 must be used in performances as indicated below. Use of the remaining cues is optional.

1. 0:42 Act One opening. (Start just before house lights dim.) Act One, Scene 1. Loud.

2. 2:07 This cue immediately follows the previous cue. (It starts as lights come up and underscores the opening scene.) Act One, Scene 1. Soft.

3. 0:13 Begin cue after this line: older Helen: " ... so we packed up what we had ... " (Underscore dialogue.) Act One, Scene 1. Soft.

4. 0:34 Begin cue after this line: Nanny: " ... Where's your apartment?" (Dialogue continues over music.) Act One, Scene 2. Soft.

5. 0:16 Begin cue after this line: Helen: "Nice and easy ... " Act One, Scene 3. Medium.

6. 0:19 Begin cue after this line: Louise: "What do you mean where's Helen?" (Dialogue continues over music.) Act One, Scene 3. Soft.

7. 0:48 Begin cue after: Nanny: " ... sticks Roger in Suzy. Now go to sleep." Act One, Scene 4. (The dialogue that follows begins when the music changes mood and continues over the rest of the music.) Medium, becoming softer when dialogue begins.

8. 1:05 Begin cue after: Jody: " ... I said stop it!" Act One, Scene 5. (the dialogue that follows begins when the music changes mood and continues over the rest of the music.) Medium going to soft when the dialogue begins.

9. 0:43 Begin cue after: Helen: "A house, Mama? Really?" (Underscores dialogue.) Act One, Scene 6. Soft.

10. 0:20 Begin cue after: Helen: " ... Joan Crawford, only better." Act One, Scene 6. Medium.

11. 0:26 Begin cue after: Louise: " ... you tell her where I am, okay?" (This music allows Helen time to get up to the roof for the next scene.) Act One, Scene 8. Medium.

12. 0:27 This cue immediately follows the previous cue, as lights come up on the next scene.(Underscores dialogue.) Act One, Scene 9. Medium, becoming soft when dialogue begins.

13. 0:31 Begin cue after: Helen: " ... I pray for you all the time." (Underscores dialogue.) Act One, Scene 9. Soft, growing louder after dialogue finishes.

14. 0:32 The cue immediately follows the previous cue. (It underscores the voice-over dialogue.) Act One, Scene 10. Soft.

15. 0:26 Begin cue after: Nanny: "Got any more harebrained schemes?" Act One, Scene 10. Medium.

16. 0:33 Begin cue at end of scene, after singing: "Live, Love, Laugh and be happy." Act One, Scene 11. Medium. The cue is faded out when the live child actors take over the singing on their entrance.

17. 0:23 Begin cue after: Louise: "You haven't got anything." (Underscores dialogue.) Act One, Scene 12. Soft.

18. 1:36 Begin cue after: Louise: "Yes." (Underscores dialogue. The action and dialogue should time to music so the Act One curtain descends as the music cue ends.) Act One, Scene 12. Soft, gradually swelling to loud at the end.

19. 0:30 Act Two opening. (Start just before house lights dim.) Act Two, Scene 1. Loud.

20. 0:23 Begin cue after: Alice: "Yes, after school." Act Two, Scene 1. Soft.

21. 0:58 Begin cue after Helen sings: " ... I never even make a gain." Act Two, Scene 2. (The actress sings the first part of "I'm Always Chasing Rainbows" with no accompaniment. At some point prior to this moment, she should be given her pitch (F#) from a pitch pipe backstage.

22. 0:40 Begin cue after: Bill: " ... sometimes we did have fun." Act Two, Scene 3. Medium.

23. 0:18 Begin cue after: Louise: "Sounds cozy as hell." (Underscores dialogue.) Act Two, Scene 4. Soft.

24. 0:28 Begin cue after: Louise: " ... hearing all those people clap like that." Act Two, Scene 4. Medium.

25. 0:33 Begin cue after: Jody: " ... I should've been the one to give you the money." Act Two, Scene 5. Medium.

26. 0:38 Begin cue after: Alice: " ... I'll sleep in the tub." Act Two, Scene 7. (During this music, Helen climbs down from the roof.) Medium.

27. 0:17 Begin cue after: Louise: "Nothing, mama." Act Two, Scene 7. Medium.

28. 0:28 Begin cue after: Louise: "It's probably for the best." (Underscores dialogue.) Act Two, Scene 8. Soft.

29. 1:03 Begin cue after: Louise: " ... we can listen to Kate Smith mooning that mountain ... "

ADDITIONAL MUSIC CUES

30. 1:32 Music for the Curtain Call. Loud.
31. 0:42 Remix of cue 1.
32. 1:38 Shorter version of cue 2.
33. 0:39 Radio Theme. (Might be playing on the radio after the announcer in Act One, Scene 2.)
34. 0:35 Remix of cue 4.
35. 0:20 Remix of cue 5.
36. 0:48 Remix of cue 7.
37. 0:55 "Red, Red Robin" on solo sax.
38. 1:06 Remix of cue 8.
39. 0:43 Remix of cue 6.
40. 0:33 Longer version of cue 10.
41. 0:25 Remix of cue 11.
42. 0:25 Variation of cue 8. (Theme for Jody.)
43. 0:41 Up tempo variation of main theme.
44. 0:31 Longer version of cue 12.
45. 1:01 Longer version of cue 15.
46. 0:23 Sax jazz solo.
47. 1:37 Remix of cue 17.
48. 0:32 Remix of cue 18.
49. 0:23 Remix of cue 19.
50. 0:58 Remix of cue 20.
51. 0:45 Different version of cue 21. (Solo piano rendition of "I'm Always Chasing Rainbows")
52. 0:34 Longer mix of cue 23.
53. 0:33 Remix of cue 24.
54. 0:39 Remix of cue 25.
55. 0:34 Longer mix of cue 26.

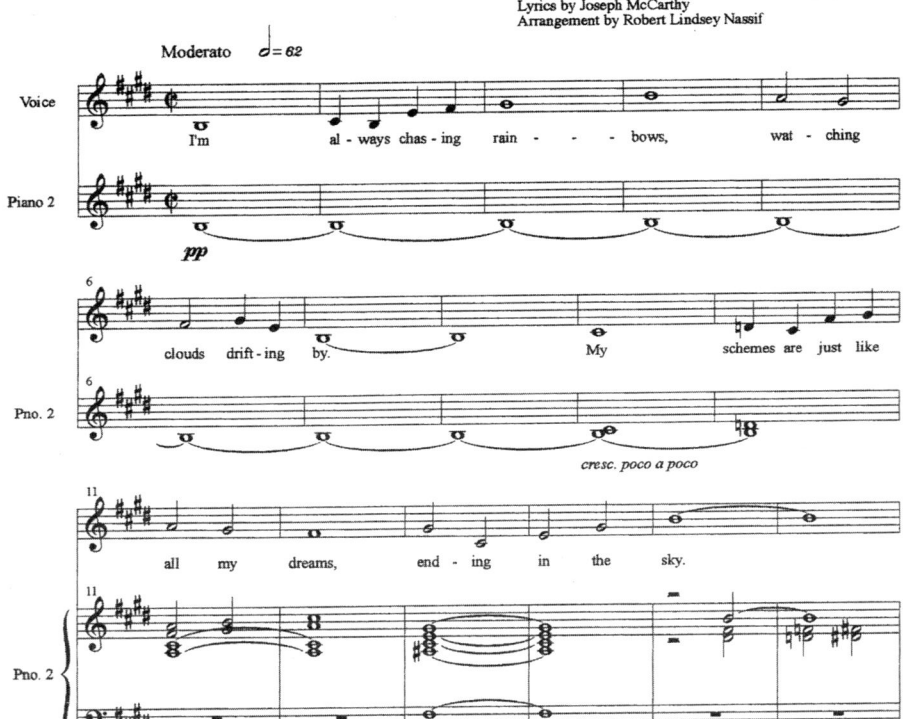

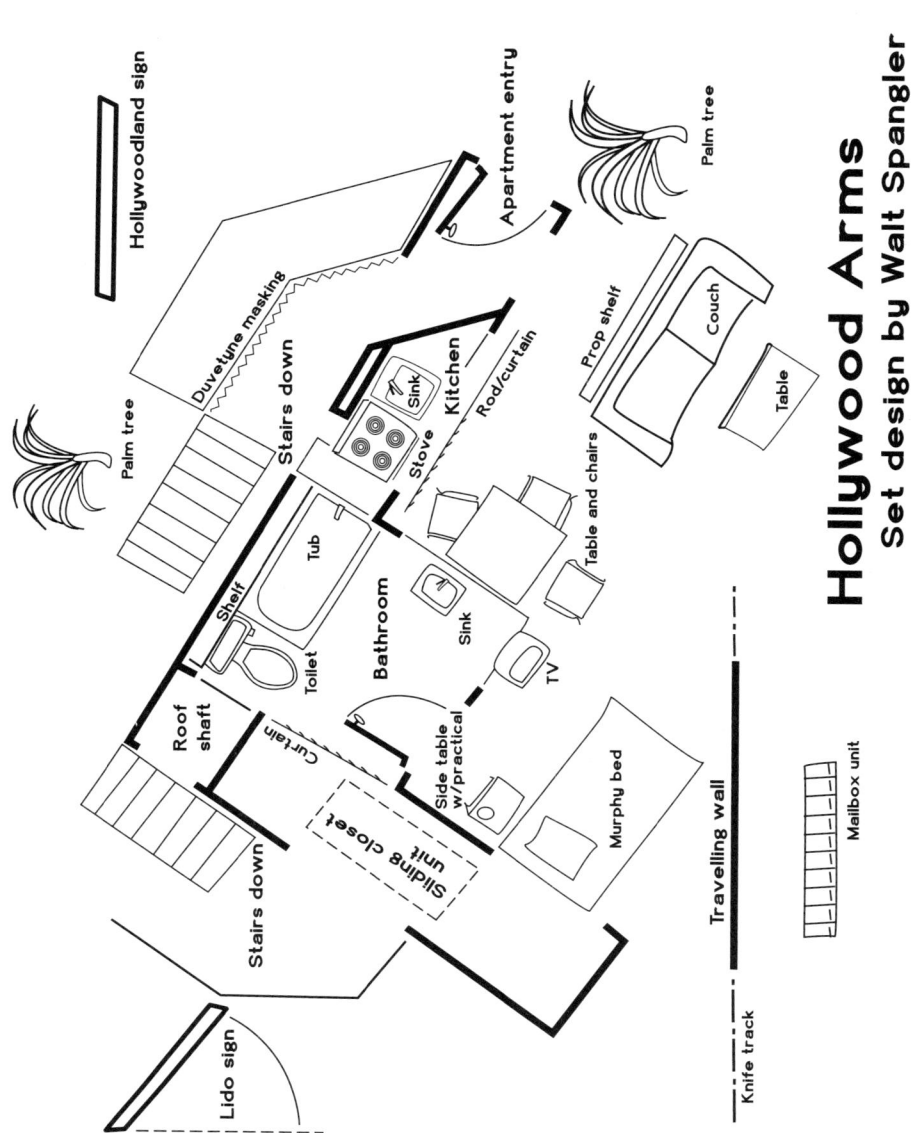

NEW PLAYS

★ **MONTHS ON END by Craig Pospisil.** In comic scenes, one for each month of the year, we follow the intertwined worlds of a circle of friends and family whose lives are poised between happiness and heartbreak. "…a triumph…these twelve vignettes all form crucial pieces in the eternal puzzle known as human relationships, an area in which the playwright displays an assured knowledge that spans deep sorrow to unbounded happiness." –*Ann Arbor News.* "…rings with emotional truth, humor…[an] endearing contemplation on love…entertaining and satisfying." –*Oakland Press.* [5M, 5W] ISBN: 0-8222-1892-5

★ **GOOD THING by Jessica Goldberg.** Brings us into the households of John and Nancy Roy, forty-something high-school guidance counselors whose marriage has been increasingly on the rocks and Dean and Mary, recent graduates struggling to make their way in life. "…a blend of gritty social drama, poetic humor and unsubtle existential contemplation…" –*Variety.* [3M, 3W] ISBN: 0-8222-1869-0

★ **THE DEAD EYE BOY by Angus MacLachlan.** Having fallen in love at their Narcotics Anonymous meeting, Billy and Shirley-Diane are striving to overcome the past together. But their relationship is complicated by the presence of Sorin, Shirley-Diane's fourteen-year-old son, a damaged reminder of her dark past. "…a grim, insightful portrait of an unmoored family…" –*NY Times.* "MacLachlan's play isn't for the squeamish, but then, tragic stories delivered at such an unrelenting fever pitch rarely are." –*Variety.* [1M, 1W, 1 boy] ISBN: 0-8222-1844-5

★ **[SIC] by Melissa James Gibson.** In adjacent apartments three young, ambitious neighbors come together to discuss, flirt, argue, share their dreams and plan their futures with unequal degrees of deep hopefulness and abject despair. "A work…concerned with the sound and power of language…" –*NY Times.* "…a wonderfully original take on urban friendship and the comedy of manners—a *Design for Living* for our times…" –*NY Observer.* [3M, 2W] ISBN: 0-8222-1872-0

★ **LOOKING FOR NORMAL by Jane Anderson.** Roy and Irma's twenty-five-year marriage is thrown into turmoil when Roy confesses that he is actually a woman trapped in a man's body, forcing the couple to wrestle with the meaning of their marriage and the delicate dynamics of family. "Jane Anderson's bittersweet transgender domestic comedy-drama …is thoughtful and touching and full of wit and wisdom. A real audience pleaser." –*Hollywood Reporter.* [5M, 4W] ISBN: 0-8222-1857-7

★ **ENDPAPERS by Thomas McCormack.** The regal Joshua Maynard, the old and ailing head of a mid-sized, family-owned book-publishing house in New York City, must name a successor. One faction in the house backs a smart, "pragmatic" manager, the other faction a smart, "sensitive" editor and both factions fear what the other's man could do to this house— and to them. "If Kaufman and Hart had undertaken a comedy about the publishing business, they might have written *Endpapers*…a breathlessly fast, funny, and thoughtful comedy …keeps you amused, guessing, and often surprised…profound in its empathy for the paradoxes of human nature." –*NY Magazine.* [7M, 4W] ISBN: 0-8222-1908-5

★ **THE PAVILION by Craig Wright.** By turns poetic and comic, romantic and philosophical, this play asks old lovers to face the consequences of difficult choices made long ago. "The script's greatest strength lies in the genuineness of its feeling." –*Houston Chronicle.* "Wright's perceptive, gently witty writing makes this familiar situation fresh and thoroughly involving." –*Philadelphia Inquirer.* [2M, 1W (flexible casting)] ISBN: 0-8222-1898-4

DRAMATISTS PLAY SERVICE, INC.
440 Park Avenue South, New York, NY 10016   212-683-8960   Fax 212-213-1539
postmaster@dramatists.com   www.dramatists.com

NEW PLAYS

★ **BE AGGRESSIVE by Annie Weisman.** Vista Del Sol is paradise, sandy beaches, avocado-lined streets. But for seventeen-year-old cheerleader Laura, everything changes when her mother is killed in a car crash, and she embarks on a journey to the Spirit Institute of the South where she can learn "cheer" with Bible belt intensity. "…filled with lingual gymnastics…stylized rapid-fire dialogue…" –*Variety*. "…a new, exciting, and unique voice in the American theatre…" –*BackStage West*. [1M, 4W, extras] ISBN: 0-8222-1894-1

★ **FOUR by Christopher Shinn.** Four people struggle desperately to connect in this quiet, sophisticated, moving drama. "…smart, broken-hearted…Mr. Shinn has a precocious and forgiving sense of how power shifts in the game of sexual pursuit…He promises to be a playwright to reckon with…" –*NY Times*. "A voice emerges from an American place. It's got humor, sadness and a fresh and touching rhythm that tell of the loneliness and secrets of life…[a] poetic, haunting play." –*NY Post*. [3M, 1W] ISBN: 0-8222-1850-X

★ **WONDER OF THE WORLD by David Lindsay-Abaire.** A madcap picaresque involving Niagara Falls, a lonely tour-boat captain, a pair of bickering private detectives and a husband's dirty little secret. "Exceedingly whimsical and playfully wicked. Winning and genial. A top-drawer production." –*NY Times*. "Full frontal lunacy is on display. A most assuredly fresh and hilarious tragicomedy of marital discord run amok…absolutely hysterical…" –*Variety*. [3M, 4W (doubling)] ISBN: 0-8222-1863-1

★ **QED by Peter Parnell.** Nobel Prize-winning physicist and all-around genius Richard Feynman holds forth with captivating wit and wisdom in this fascinating biographical play that originally starred Alan Alda. "QED is a seductive mix of science, human affections, moral courage, and comic eccentricity. It reflects on, among other things, death, the absence of God, travel to an unexplored country, the pleasures of drumming, and the need to know and understand." –*NY Magazine*. "Its rhythms correspond to the way that people—even geniuses—approach and avoid highly emotional issues, and it portrays Feynman with affection and awe." –*The New Yorker*. [1M, 1W] ISBN: 0-8222-1924-7

★ **UNWRAP YOUR CANDY by Doug Wright.** Alternately chilling and hilarious, this deliciously macabre collection of four bedtime tales for adults is guaranteed to keep you awake for nights on end. "Engaging and intellectually satisfying…a treat to watch." –*NY Times*. "Fiendishly clever. Mordantly funny and chilling. Doug Wright teases, freezes and zaps us." –*Village Voice*. "Four bite-size plays that bite back." –*Variety*. [flexible casting] ISBN: 0-8222-1871-2

★ **FURTHER THAN THE FURTHEST THING by Zinnie Harris.** On a remote island in the middle of the Atlantic secrets are buried. When the outside world comes calling, the islanders find their world blown apart from the inside as well as beyond. "Harris winningly produces an intimate and poetic, as well as political, family saga." –*Independent (London)*. "Harris' enthralling adventure of a play marks a departure from stale, well-furrowed theatrical terrain." –*Evening Standard (London)*. [3M, 2W] ISBN: 0-8222-1874-7

★ **THE DESIGNATED MOURNER by Wallace Shawn.** The story of three people living in a country where what sort of books people like to read and how they choose to amuse themselves becomes both firmly personal and unexpectedly entangled with questions of survival. "This is a playwright who does not just tell you what it is like to be arrested at night by goons or to fall morally apart and become an aimless yet weirdly contented ghost yourself. He has the originality to make you feel it." –*Times (London)*. "A fascinating play with beautiful passages of writing…" –*Variety*. [2M, 1W] ISBN: 0-8222-1848-8

DRAMATISTS PLAY SERVICE, INC.
440 Park Avenue South, New York, NY 10016 212-683-8960 Fax 212-213-1539
postmaster@dramatists.com   www.dramatists.com

NEW PLAYS

★ **SHEL'S SHORTS by Shel Silverstein.** Lauded poet, songwriter and author of children's books, the incomparable Shel Silverstein's short plays are deeply infused with the same wicked sense of humor that made him famous. "...[a] childlike honesty and twisted sense of humor." *–Boston Herald.* "...terse dialogue and an absurdity laced with a tang of dread give [*Shel's Shorts*] more than a trace of Samuel Beckett's comic existentialism." *–Boston Phoenix.* [flexible casting] ISBN: 0-8222-1897-6

★ **AN ADULT EVENING OF SHEL SILVERSTEIN by Shel Silverstein.** Welcome to the darkly comic world of Shel Silverstein, a world where nothing is as it seems and where the most innocent conversation can turn menacing in an instant. These ten imaginative plays vary widely in content, but the style is unmistakable. "...[*An Adult Evening*] shows off Silverstein's virtuosic gift for wordplay...[and] sends the audience out...with a clear appreciation of human nature as perverse and laughable." *–NY Times.* [flexible casting] ISBN: 0-8222-1873-9

★ **WHERE'S MY MONEY? by John Patrick Shanley.** A caustic and sardonic vivisection of the institution of marriage, laced with the author's inimitable razor-sharp wit. "...Shanley's gift for acid-laced one-liners and emotionally tumescent exchanges is certainly potent..." *–Variety.* "...lively, smart, occasionally scary and rich in reverse wisdom." *–NY Times.* [3M, 3W] ISBN: 0-8222-1865-8

★ **A FEW STOUT INDIVIDUALS by John Guare.** A wonderfully screwy comedy-drama that figures Ulysses S. Grant in the throes of writing his memoirs, surrounded by a cast of fantastical characters, including the Emperor and Empress of Japan, the opera star Adelina Patti and Mark Twain. "Guare's smarts, passion and creativity skyrocket to awesome heights..." *–Star Ledger.* "...precisely the kind of good new play that you might call an everyday miracle...every minute of it is fresh and newly alive..." *–Village Voice.* [10M, 3W] ISBN: 0-8222-1907-7

★ **BREATH, BOOM by Kia Corthron.** A look at fourteen years in the life of Prix, a Bronx native, from her ruthless girl-gang leadership at sixteen through her coming to maturity at thirty. "...vivid world, believable and eye-opening, a place worthy of a dramatic visit, where no one would want to live but many have to." *–NY Times.* "...rich with humor, terse vernacular strength and gritty detail..." *–Variety.* [1M, 9W] ISBN: 0-8222-1849-6

★ **THE LATE HENRY MOSS by Sam Shepard.** Two antagonistic brothers, Ray and Earl, are brought together after their father, Henry Moss, is found dead in his seedy New Mexico home in this classic Shepard tale. "...His singular gift has been for building mysteries out of the ordinary ingredients of American family life..." *–NY Times.* "...rich moments ...Shepard finds gold." *–LA Times.* [7M, 1W] ISBN: 0-8222-1858-5

★ **THE CARPETBAGGER'S CHILDREN by Horton Foote.** One family's history spanning from the Civil War to WWII is recounted by three sisters in evocative, intertwining monologues. "...bittersweet music—[a] rhapsody of ambivalence...in its modest, garrulous way...theatrically daring." *–The New Yorker.* [3W] ISBN: 0-8222-1843-7

★ **THE NINA VARIATIONS by Steven Dietz.** In this funny, fierce and heartbreaking homage to *The Seagull*, Dietz puts Chekhov's star-crossed lovers in a room and doesn't let them out. "A perfect little jewel of a play..." *–Shepherdstown Chronicle.* "...a delightful revelation of a writer at play; and also an odd, haunting, moving theater piece of lingering beauty." *–Eastside Journal (Seattle).* [1M, 1W (flexible casting)] ISBN: 0-8222-1891-7

DRAMATISTS PLAY SERVICE, INC.
440 Park Avenue South, New York, NY 10016   212-683-8960   Fax 212-213-1539
postmaster@dramatists.com   www.dramatists.com